D1555480

BACK
TO THE
GHETTO

BACK TO THE GHETTO

ZIONISM IN RETREAT

URI HUPPERT

BM
390
.H87
1988
West

PROMETHEUS BOOKS
Buffalo, New York

BACK TO THE GHETTO: ZIONISM IN RETREAT. Copyright © 1988 by Uri Huppert. All rights reserved. Printed in the United States of America. No part of this book may be reproduced in any manner whatsoever without written permission, except in the case of brief quotations embodied in critical articles and reviews. Inquiries should be addressed to Prometheus Books, 700 East Amherst Street, Buffalo, New York 14215.

91 90 89 88   4 3 2 1

Library of Congress Cataloging-in-Publication Data

Huppert, Uri, 1932-
    Back to the ghetto.

    Bibliography: p. 229
    1. Religion and state—Israel. 2. Orthodox Judaism—Israel.
3. Nationalism—Israel—Religious aspects—Judaism. 4. Religious
Zionism—Israel. 5. Israel—Politics and government.
6. Israel—ethnic relations. I. Title.
BM390.H87   1988   322′.1′095694   88-15105
ISBN 0-87975-467-2

This book is dedicated to my sons, Roy and Eran, and to their peers. May doubt alone gnaw at their hearts. May they not fall prey to the absolute truths in whose name deranged minds have in the past sowed seeds of poison, destruction, suffering and terror.

Table of Contents

*"I was a paratrooper fighting at Beirut airport. . . .
The bullets were screaming past me, but I wasn't as
scared of that Lebanese inferno as I was of Fridays
in Mea Shearim in Jerusalem."*

> —Daniel Saban, Israeli policeman seriously in-
> jured by ultra-Orthodox haredi Jews while
> protecting a tourist couple being assaulted
> by ultra-Orthodox Jews in Jerusalem
> (*Ma'ariv,* 25 August 1985)

Preface

The book before the reader is significantly influenced by the horrors of the Holocaust. As a child born to Jewish parents in Upper Silesia in Poland, on the eve of Hitler's rise to power, it was my fate to personally experience the rule of National Socialism.

Even before the outbreak of World War II, the German minority in Silesia began arrogantly declaring its empathy with Hitler's adoration of the "superior" Aryan race. These disclosures were received with forgiveness. By September 17, 1939, the Ribentrop-Molotov Agreement had brought Stalin's regime into Central Europe. Arrests had begun, coupled with the transfer of "unwanted elements" to Siberia and Soviet Asia. Families were torn apart, exiled, and shot.

The Holocaust, ghettos, concentration camps, and mass murders turned the annihilation of a nation into a "legitimate" cause. The liberation of Central and Eastern Europe from the claws of the Nazis reawakened the threat of a Stalinistic rule in the consciousness of the Free World.

My formative years were spent under totalitarian regimes. The fear that this phenomenon would return under a different name in another place was not mine alone.

I owe special thanks to the great Polish poet in exile, Czeslaw Milosz, who for many years dedicated himself to the study of the captive mind. Milosz tells the fictional story of Murti-Bing, a Mongolian philosopher who succeeded in creating a potion containing within it a certain "outlook on life." Several pills were enough to make one "repent" and become part of this "desirable" lifestyle. The "repenter" was "blessed" with ecstasy and well-being and lost all ability for freedom of thought. From this point on, he was. the vessel in the hands of the regime, led by a totalitarian ideology.

The experiences of my youth under two regimes, each one in its own way representing absolute justice and exclusive solutions, has left its scars. For many years I feared disclosing this fact, believing it was my mark of Cain, which separated me from my "normal" peers who had the good fortune of having been born in another, less traumatic part of the globe.

I finally came to understand that this scar is a sign and symbol of a universal experience. I came to understand that inasmuch as it is legitimate to share the illusions of war, the troubles of life in general, and the agony of love with others, so is it legitimate for one to present before his friends one's scars as proof of having actually passed through the seven gates of hell.

The scars of this hell sensitized me to all symptoms of totalitarianism. These scars and these sensitivities were a major factor in the writing of this book—a book dealing with Israeli reality that, on the face of it, makes no claim to Murti-Bing or others like him.

Would that the reader, as he or she turns the final page, might be able to say: Put your fears to rest. Between Murti-

Bing and what is taking place in Israel there is no resemblance, none at all.

Acknowledgments

I am very grateful to Professor Lawrence Kaplan, Director of the Lyman L. Lemnitzer Center for NATO Studies, Dr. Abraham Peck, Director of the American Jewish Archives (H.U.C.), and Professor Saul Friedman, Youngstown University, for their encouragement and support; and to Rabbi M.R. from Jerusalem, for his precious remarks.

Introduction

Israeli society today is no longer merely threatened by the specter of a Kulturkampf between the goals of religious Orthodoxy and those of the Jewish state. It is now an unhappy reality.

The ultra-Orthodox extremists—the non-Zionist Agudat Yisrael and the anti-Zionist haredi groups—deflect the public's view of the situation, so that the ultra-Orthodox appear responsible for the present extremism. In fact, however, it was the "moderate," religious-Zionist parties—Mizrachi, Poel Mizrachi, and their successor, the National Religious Party (NRP)—that brought about the present situation, even if it doesn't fully profit from it today.

The NRP and its predecessors have had a long association with the Zionist movement and have been granted special privileges by it almost from the beginning. These privileges were the forerunners of today's coalition agreements. Already in 1920, Mizrachi was given autonomy in educational matters by the World Zionist Organization. From this developed the seeds of the public-religious school system; Kibbutz Dati, the Orthodox-religious Kibbutz movement; and Oz V'Shalom; as well as "Gush Emunim," the Bloc of the Faithful; and the clerical-nationalistic messianic movement.

Already in 1934, the Jewish National Fund was required to insert a paragraph mandating Sabbath observance in all leases for new settlements. In 1935, recognition of Sabbath observance was demanded from the Mandate Government. Mizrachi, and later the NRP, proceeded to set up alternative Orthodox-religious institutions parallel to those established by the Yishuv, and afterwards the State, in all spheres of life:

1. The system of religious courts was preserved and developed in opposition to the secular system of courts by virtue of the Jurisdiction of the Rabbinical Courts Act of 1953.

2. The public-religious educational system, which inculcates Orthodox religious ideology, was established opposite the secular system by the Public Education Act of 1953.

3. Local Jewish religious councils were established opposite secular municipal authorities.

4. An extremist Orthodox-religious ideology was established in opposition to the democratic Zionist vision embodied in Israel's Declaration of Independence.[1]

Miriam Levinger, wife of Gush Emunim Rabbi Moshe Levinger, expressed the extremist attitude now prevalent in the Orthodox religious-nationalist camp in her well-known remark that "democracy is not a Jewish value." And in fact roadblocks are set up on the Sabbath in violation of freedom of movement, and economic pressure is exerted on places of entertainment by the Rabbinate by virtue of the authority granted to it by the secular Knesset, in violation of freedom of cultural activity.

Long before the issue reached its present proportions, Orthodoxy also became the dominant voice for dormant ethnicity. It was largely due to Orthodox pressure that some sovereign state structures and systems financed by the state budget became institutionalized on ethnic lines.

The rabbinical tribunals are openly based on the principle of ethnic balance. It is there that the division between Sephardi and Ashkenazi is sharply emphasized. The separation is presented as the legacy of Ottoman rule, but it is in fact a direct expression of Orthodox policy.

The Orthodox approach enabled the establishment of the two-headed Chief Rabbinate, leading to a kind of Jewish Orthodox "Episcopalian church."

State funds were not distributed to the Reform synagogues, which avoid blatant ethnic division, but they were poured into Orthodox synagogues and institutions, including burial societies, which manifest sharply defined ethnic divisions. The Jewish Israeli is inextricably entangled in these divisions from birth to death.

Ethnic divisions are so deeply ingrained that they have lasted through successive generations. Indeed, well-established clerical enterprises are based solely on this ethnic separation. It can well be said that the strength of Orthodoxy itself was enhanced by the emphasis on ethnic division, and perhaps even allowed certain developments that, ironically, have now turned against it. It is no coincidence that the Tami party, the mainly North African ethnic religious movement, was led by Aharon Abu-Hatzeira, a former distinguished member of the NRP executive branch and a former member of the Israeli cabinet, who held the religious affairs portfolio as the representative of Zionist Orthodoxy in the government. Then, too, there is the phenomenon of messianic nationalism, which spawned Gush Emunim, the Morasha movement (Knesset member Rabbi Haim Druckman), and Kach, all of which can be traced directly to the determination of the NRP to permit, even to enable, the development of differences of opinion so long as they remained within the Orthodox camp. Rabbi Israel Ariel, one of the most vociferous adherents of Rabbi Meir Kahane, openly declared that he was merely following the path of the mother party—the NRP.

The Orthodoxy led by the "good guys" of the NRP affected medicine (by restricting autopsy); industry, transportation, and entertainment (by restricting Shabes activities); burials (by monopolizing funerals and cemeteries); the food industry (by Kashruth—religious ritual, dietary restrictions); the military (by creating exceptional options for women who declare their religious-Orthodox affiliation and men who enroll in Yeshiva, enter religious-Orthodox units, or join as cadets in the religious-Orthodox Military Academy); local governments (by establishing concurrent Jewish religious councils); and family life (by monopolizing marriages and divorces). The "good guys" claim they have nothing to do with religious coercion: They are not committing acts of coercion because they are changing the very structure of the State of Israel step by step with patience and without physical brutality.

The NRP claims only two marginal factors are to be blamed for the "sudden" deterioration in the "excellent" relationship between Orthodoxy and the "others": the physical violence exercised by irrational ultra-Orthodox minor groups, and the "antireligious" prejudice of "ignorant" secularists. The Zionist Orthodoxy asks for sympathy while considering itself the "good Orthodox guys."

In fact, however, the mostly sophisticated "moderate" religious-Orthodox Zionism—ideologically led by Rabbi Shlomo Goren, Rabbi Moshe Tzvi Neriah, and many others, and politically represented by Mizrachi and Poel Mizrachi (known later as the NRP) brought about the present situation not only by sanctioning the poor dualistic legal system in Orthodox hands but also by usurping the Law of Return and enforcing a quasi-religious definition in the infamous issue of "who is a Jew." (By the same token they avoided any recognition of non-Orthodox religious Jews.)

The Zionist religious Orthodoxy, not the ultra-Orthodox haredi groups, created an establishment in four parts: (a) rabbinical, by reconfirming an Orthodox Jewish Episcopal church, the Chief Rabbinate; (b) judicial, by safeguarding the rabbinical Orthodox monopoly in family courts; (c) educational, by creating a separate public religious school system under Orthodox auspices and following an Orthodox curriculum; (d) political, by establishing Orthodox representation in the National Parliament (the Knesset), in local governments, and in local Jewish religious councils, which are heavily influenced by the Orthodoxy.

Thus, the Orthodoxy in Israel is no longer only a creed; it is a well-established clerical rabbinical hierarchy and lay political and administrative infrastructure affecting very strongly the most sensitive political issues.

The ethnic unrest that spread over Israel in the last decade created a new dimension to Orthodoxy as an "authentic" Jewish response to Western-minded secular Ashkenazi politicians. In addition, many Orthodox voters, swayed by the charismatic nationalistic leadership of Menachem Begin, switched to the Likud party.

Now, a generation after the Six Day War, nationalistic-Zionist Orthodoxy has emerged as a "nationalized" Talmudic-halachic ideology of the Israeli "Moral Majority." This trend represents almost 50 percent of the Israeli electorate if we mention only the Likud, the Tehiah, the Kach (Meir Kahane's representation), and the historic Orthodox political parties.

Not everybody in this bracket is a Zionist, and not everybody holds Orthodox beliefs either, but almost all of them are ready to accept similar political goals as far as the concept of "Greater Israel" is concerned and to pay for it by benefiting the Orthodoxy. Additional issues of mutual interest exist, such as national uniformism; "purity" of the people of Israel; cultural puritan curriculum; antagonism toward leftist intellectuals and journalists who are "controlling" the media and "destroying" the structure of Jewish life in the Jewish state; and safeguarding of the separation between Jews and Gentiles (mainly Arabs).

The late Vladimir Jabotinsky never lost his position as the "Great Chaplain" of the Revisionist Movement—which gave birth to the Herut faction, the dominant factor in the Likud bloc—but who really knows his ideology?[2] In practical terms, this secular nationalistic leader's opinions are no longer needed; they are even confusing. (Jabotinsky's son, Professor Ery Jabotinsky, was active in the anticlerical League Against Religious Coercion in Israel.)

The Nationalistic camp, strongly influenced by messianic-fundamentalistic religious-Orthodoxy, pays lip service to Jabotinsky, using him as a leading common denominator of the Israeli Right. It is only natural that the Right should express emotional and political understanding toward Orthodox religious demands while having no moral or political obligations toward the non-Orthodox, mainly liberal, and even anticlerical Jews in America, who are so sensitive to universal issues of freedom and equality, and who are frequently critical of Israeli domestic and international affairs.

This newly born Israeli right-wing establishment is developing good relations with the American Orthodox minority. This American Orthodoxy is expressing its growing appreciation to the American right wing as well.[3]

— 1 —

Escape from the Ghetto

The aim of European Jews to leave the ghetto was received by the Christian ruling society with great skepticism. However, the Jews themselves had fanatically preserved the physical walls of the ghetto and eyed interreligious and intercommunal tolerance with growing suspicion.

With the end of Moses Mendelssohn's era in Germany, in the late eighteenth century, the enlightened Gentile society was prepared for discussions and meetings with the Jews, but the average Gentile people, who spread throughout Europe from Poland to England, were very apprehensive. The blending of Jews in their communal life was not acceptable to them.

Jewish Orthodoxy had no differences of opinion with these Gentiles; it was completely against the process of convergence and even worked to build up the ghetto walls. Furthermore, escape of Jewish youth from the ghetto framework was viewed as treachery, according to the Jewish traditional-Orthodox value system. Escape proclaimed the crumbling of the Jewish community and was defined as a deviation from the legitimate course of Jewish history.[1]

The process of Jewish integration into the intellectual life of the West, however, introduced secular studies, such as literature and the sciences, into Jewish life. The entrance of Jews into the sciences, literature, philosophy, plastic arts, and the theater contributed greatly, both in quantity and quality, to European culture.

Subsequent to the French Revolution (1789) and Poland's three divisions (1772-95), and following changes in Holland's legislation (1795), Jewish emancipation was an undisputed fact for all Europeans, Gentiles and Jews alike.

From the Jewish Orthodox point of view, however, even the legitimate connections with the Gentiles were not what they had been. The "Jews of the courtyard" were awarded recognition of their identity by Gentile rulers, and the commercial interaction between the two groups surpassed the strict framework of buyer-seller connections. The sophisticated economy created not only a complex commercial relationship but also an intricate system of human relations. Distinguished Jewish families, such as the Arensteins in Vienna, were active behind the scenes during the Congress of Vienna (1814-15) and created a Jewish lobby for the protection of Jewish civil rights. The Rothschild family's success followed the Arenstein family's experiment. It became apparent to all that Judaism could not continue to survive as a closed, segregated sect and that a basic change of character was vital for the Jews' continued existence under the rapidly changing conditions.

The minority remained in the European ghettos, while the decisive majority of Jews broke through the barrier that the Gentile world on one hand and Orthodox Jewry on the other had built around them. They poured new substance into Judaism, which has enabled the existence of both the isolated Jew and Judaism as an ethnic group to this day.

The nationalist anti-Zionist version of Judasim (the Bund) developed alongside Zionism as the Jewish equivalent of the explosion of European nationalism as expressed by Garibaldi's nationalist movement in Italy, the Polish intellectual and military renaissance, the American War of Independence, the Jacobin Revolution, and the growth of Socialism.

Thus, the Jewish religious non-Orthodox currents were born, and on the eve of the Holocaust, the majority of German Jews, who had until then adhered to their religious Judaism, departed from the Orthodoxy.

Zionism, which desired a renewal of Jewish nationalism, collided head-on with the Reform Jews, who abrogated national identity and held only to a religious creed. Simultaneously, Zionism collided with religious Orthodoxy, which protested the human construction of national independence in the Holy Land (opposing human construction of the Third Temple). Thanks to European influence, and in contradiction to Islam, the Jewish people experienced a kind of "Jewish Reformation," which gave birth to a variety of political and social philosophies as well as theologies:

> Two main movements proved their vitality while imbibing the Western culture and attempting to normalize the Jews distorted by ghettoic life. The Reform religious movement did it by rejecting unhumanistic concepts anchored in some Talmudic-Halachic (Orthodox) teachings, and by assimilation into the nation of domicile, as a religion. The political Zionism—the national Jewish movement—did it by rejecting the Orthodox concept of Ethnocentric national entity guided by Divine Law specifically

stipulated by the Almighty God for his chosen people and by colliding with religious Orthodoxy, which protested the human construction of national independence in the Holy Land (opposing human construction of the Third Temple). Zionism advocated assimilation into the family of nations as a sovereign statehood and by accepting the newly born modern secular, policentric nationalism.[2]

A minute portion of the Orthodox minority, which was repelled by the mainstream of Orthodoxy and protested the Reform and Conservative Jewish theologies, jumped on the wagon of Zionism and impressed its growing mark upon it.

— 2 —
From State Sovereignty
to Rabbinical Entity

Orthodoxy and Democracy

Rabbi Haim Hirschensohn, born in the kabbalists' town of Safad, never strayed from his early path, nor from his identification with the Orthodox stream—rather the opposite.[1] He regarded himself as one of the founders of the Zionist-religious Mizrachi movement, which later appeared on the Israeli political scene as the National Religious Party (NRP).

The good rabbi, however, was condemned as a maverick. A native-born Israeli and a lifelong adherent of Orthodox theology, he was nonetheless forced to leave the land of his physical and spiritual birth to seek sanctuary in the United States. No fault was found with him there, and until his death he served as rabbi of an Orthodox congregation in New Jersey.

Indeed, Hirschensohn's biographer Eliezer Schweid suggests that a deliberate attempt was made to distance the rabbi from his party's main institutions.

What was Rabbi Hirschensohn's crime? What were his views, and how did they differ from Orthodoxy?

It cannot be denied that in his prolific writings Rabbi Hirschensohn dealt at length with democratic rule in the Jewish state, dwelling on his hopes that it would indeed come about. He was convinced that the Zionist movement, colored as it was by Western philosophy and thought, would enable the secular Jew to breach religious barriers and attain democracy in the Jewish state. Hirschensohn himself was an ardent devotee of democracy; his convictions were strengthened by his difficulties in Palestine and his experience in the United States. Where did the crime lie? Rabbi Hirshensohn was convinced that if Orthodoxy did not develop "a Torah [Religious] democracy as an act of grace from the God of Israel," secular Zionism would establish democratic rule fashioned in the Western mode. Then there would be no escape from a collision between the two philosophical approaches. Schweid notes that "in any case, democracy as commanded in the Torah cannot be identical to democracy as it is understood within a secular framework, because secular democracy is after all based on the sovereignty of manmade institutions within the scope of the law. . . . We are speaking of a democracy based on the laws of God and not the laws of man."[2]

This approach apparently did not find favor with the rabbinical establishment. It is, after all, from the Gemara, or oral law, that we have the aphorism, "an evil connection must not be considered." The essence of this phrase is that the concept of "majority" has no constitutional value in itself. Talmudic Judaism is based on an elitist approach of the superiority of Torah knowledge. Mystical worth and quality are the determining factors—not quantity.

The Babylonian Talmud describes the dispute that broke out among the leaders of the group headed by Hezekiah.[3] Shabna the scribe led the majority group among the people, and he advocated surrender to the Assyrians. This was opposed by the king, who led the minority opinion, and indeed, his opinion prevailed—a decision that brought fame to him and to the entire people of Israel. True wisdom interprets this tale as illustrating the folly of always accepting a majority decision in any situation merely because it is the majority. The opposite, in fact, is the wise course. Under certain circumstances, the Torah commands that when the majority "digresses from the ways of the Torah," that decision should be unequivocally rejected. The Talmudic approach is consistent. Imbued with the grace of God, the leaders—the Talmudic scholars—decide the fate of the individual, and not the majority, which may well be evil as it has digressed from the path of the Torah.

In the circumstances, Rabbi Hirschensohn's approach was rejected in its entirety, even though he only observed that "totalitarian democracy" that was not accepted by the majority should be followed only when it expressed divine intention.

The Orthodox camp, however, did not abandon the issue when it came to secular rule. In the Diaspora, where the Jew has no choice but to obey the rule of manmade law, it has been determined that the law of the land is binding. The Jew obeys instructions and also accedes to the demands of the ruler. However, if the ruler gave the Jews limited autonomy—and such instances have been recorded since the Middle Ages—Jewish judges were permitted to sit on the bench, and the verdict was left to the Jews themselves.

It is one of the ironies of certain versions of Jewish

Orthodoxy that as long as a Jew is to obey a foreign rule exercised by Gentiles, he must accept it, even if unwillingly. But when members of a Jewish community did acquire limited self-rule, the problem of accepting this partially Jewish rule became more difficult. For example, what about a Jewish judge in a Gentile court? Precisely where did the Jewish judge diverge from foreign law, or even Israeli secular law, contradicting the Talmudic-halachic Orthodox religious legal concept? At what point did the judge say, "Enough! From this point on I will not conform. I will judge my people according to Talmudic law." In terms of the rabbinical vocabulary, does the law of the land apply in its entirety, or should the judge, in certain spheres, give preference to the Gemara and hence challenge the sovereign authority? Should the Jewish judge, a member of a closed and isolated Orthodox community, obey state rule or obey the rabbinate? Talmudic literature, like a fountain, sends up a spray of divergent solutions.

Orthodoxy transferred this uncertainty to the judiciary of the State of Israel. Doubts multiplied, and the dispute intensified. Jewish judges now sit on the judicial bench in a Jewish state and judge the Jewish citizens of that state according to laws enacted by a secular, elected parliament. Should an observant Jew obey a law of the Jews that does not emanate from Talmudic sources and occasionally contradicts the Talmudic approach in essential issues? There are many examples, such as equal rights for women; prohibition of marriage between a boy and a girl who have reached, respectively, the ages of 13 and 12; and acknowledgment of the equal rights of Gentiles. The problem goes even deeper. Is it even necessary, indeed permissible, for a Jew who observes the Torah and follows the Commandments to obey these courts at all? Can a Jew sit on the bench in circumstances like this? If he does, is he under secular sovereign authority, or will a Talmudic edict be found to justify the issue because of "lack of choice"? This leads, of course, to the premise that a Jewish judge of religious Orthodox orientation may not in fact recognize the full sovereignty of the secular legislative body.

For extremist, anti-Zionist Orthodoxy, there are no doubts. The State of Israel is not recognized and is regarded as an expression of false messianism. The State is rejected precisely because it emanates from Jews. Extremist Orthodoxy wins on both counts. It does not recognize the sovereignty of Zionist rule and simultaneously rejects a secular judiciary. It regards the law of the land as legitimate only when pronounced by a Gentile ruler—certainly not when the ruler is a deviant Jew who in principle is a heretic, denying that only God will build the Third Temple.

This group includes the Neturei Karta sect; the spiritual leaders, teachers, and students of Jerusalem's Toldot Aharon yeshiva (seminary); and the followers of the Szatmar rabbi. The reasoning of Agudat Yisrael and Shas followers on one hand, and that of Zionist Orthodoxy on the other, is rather more complicated. Their nationalist-religious faith enables them to accept as binding the secular laws of the State of Israel, although they have reservations about legislation that contradicts Talmudic halacha. It is here that the Orthodox camp wants to leave its mark on the constitutional structure of the state of the Jews. While it opposes the secular structure of the state, it nevertheless is prepared to grant it limited legitimacy in order to acquire an authentic voice in its affairs.

Institutes for the Research of Talmudic Law affiliated with the secular universities and Talmudic research institutes like the Ha'Rav Kook Institute, Bar Ilan University, and yeshiva colleges have unearthed a vast amount of material. Also well known is the decision of the Supreme Rabbinical Appeal

Tribunal that even in the Holy Land secular law is binding, on condition that it does not contradict halachic strictures.

Superficially, this may appear to be a winning point for sovereign law in Israel—a partial recognition of Knesset law by the opposing establishment—but in practice it is no victory. The recognition is limited. The rabbinical tribunals, which exist by grace of the secular legislature, are in no hurry to respect their progenitor. The rivalry between the two systems is sadly evident.

The Knesset tamely accepted its lack of control over the rabbinical legal system and even gave it statutory legitimacy.

Section 10 of the Rabbinical Judges Act specifically frees rabbinical judges officiating in family (rabbinical) tribunals from taking an oath of allegiance to the laws of the State.[4] To the contrary, the rabbinical establishment, which exists only by grace of the laws of the State, struck out against those very laws. Rabbi Herzog, the extremely influential chief rabbi at the time of the establishment of the State, denied the civil judiciary, saying that it "tramples upon the Torah of the living God."[5] Even during a national rabbinical conference the intellectual abilities of the judges were decried: "Men who are ignorant in Talmudic halacha want to judge Torah scholars according to the laws of the Gentiles."[6]

Orthodoxy's concept of sovereignty and the democratic concept of majority rule are not compatible, and Rabbi Hirschensohn's attempts to sugar the pill by presenting the Torah in a modern context did not bridge the gap between the two schools of thought. The identical situation holds today.

Nevertheless, Talmudic opposition to democracy as an expression of the people's sovereignty does not emphasize the contradiction.

Significant sectors in Orthodoxy are prepared to play the parliamentary game according to the obligations of democratic authority. But they hedge that willingness by demanding predetermined rules. It is an unwritten understanding that the delegates will democratically adopt Orthodox concepts, thus making a mockery of majority vote. It was by this means that the religious parties representing Orthodoxy joined the not-so-exclusive club of political parties with a totalitarian approach. They carried out their aims by unilateral playing of the parliamentary game. It was as if they said: "We will support the democratic process so long as it allows legislation and agreements according to our way of thought, and we will oppose it completely if it does not serve our purpose."

Unfortunately, and with infinite regret, it must be acknowledged that this indeed happens. Totalitarian movements in Europe have successfully destroyed the rule of law and established a new order, and have even enacted racist laws by majority vote.

It is an odious comparison, but history records that the Nuremberg Laws were passed in Germany without in any way impinging on the authority of the legislation of the Weimar Republic. This demonstrates that democratic action does not necessarily express democratic content. It is merely a mold that pre-forms the legislative establishment duly elected by the entire enfranchised population. This establishment then is a sovereign body that can and does create legislation. The character and content of the legislation depends not on the method of voting but rather on the self-imposed restraints of the legislative body to prevent the passage of specific decisions. Since majority rule holds sway, each decision is indisputably democratic.

The Nazis were perfectly right in insisting on the democratic origin of the Nuremberg Laws, claiming that their actual passage through the Bundestag was in strict accordance with democratic rules. Israeli laws relating to personal status that have an adverse effect on certain sectors of the population are not, as is frequently claimed, undemocratic. Similarly, a law prohibiting the eating in public of leavened bread during Passover is not undemocratic.[7] The practical measure of democracy is no more than a mechanical count of votes in the legislature. This is the direct reason for the defense mechanisms that democratic entities have built into their constitutions even more strongly since World War II. These enable them to avoid committing democratic suicide.

A defended democracy is one with enough built-in checks and balances to prevent individual political groups that oppose the rule of law from overthrowing that democracy, while still playing the democratic game strictly according to the rules.

A decision-making apparatus, therefore, is an additional dimension of democracy, and that dimension is the rule of law.

Some prominent Talmudic scholars summarize their stand on the secular judicial system this way.[8] The authority of the system lies in the laws of the Israeli Knesset. In the secular Jewish courts judgment is rendered according to Ottoman and British laws, still a legacy from the checkered past of this beleaguered country, or laws renewed in the Israeli Knesset. Hence the judgment is like that of all Gentile courts, and unless the litigant bluntly refuses to accept their authority, this authority passes to the rabbinical courts. Only after these courts have rendered their judgment will the litigant, with the added stricture of having to observe the Commandments, be permitted to be judged in a secular court.

Democratic rule of this elective nature is expressed by open elections in which any adult citizen may participate without restriction on religion, nationality (*le'om* in Hebrew), ethnic origin, race, or sex. The citizens choose a legislature, which is the sole authority with the power of legislation. It is by this method that democracy becomes a parliamentary democracy. But this is not enough. The parliament guards its independence by making its actions conditional. That condition is the rule of law. This means that no legislation is enacted that could impinge upon the rule of law in Israel.

The essential principle of the rule of law is that the State was proposed in order neither to enforce conceptual norms nor to determine regulations that enforce a specific ideology. The rule of law prevents the enactment of uniform ideological, theological, spiritual norms—that is to say, totalitarian thought. The rule of law does not permit legislation that makes Marxism the only scientific approach for the education of the next generation or the norm by which writers express themselves. The meaning of the rule of law is that belief and the lack of belief are not subjects for legislation.

The democratic tradition of the Western world does not acknowledge any compromise on these issues. Article 10 of the 1789 French Declaration of the Rights of Man states that no person will be harmed because of personal views or religious approach. The First Amendment of the 1791 American Bill of Rights proscribes the power of Congress to legislate "on freedom of expression and religion." Backed by bitter experience, the Federal Republic of Germany in 1949 enacted a basic law promising freedom of conscience, faith, and ideological expression. The United Nations on December 10, 1948, published a declaration of human rights clearly outlining the principle of freedom of thought and religion. On a broader basis, we have the decisions of the 1966 International Convention on the Elimination of All Forms of Racial Discrimination, and the European Convention on Human Rights. The U.S. Congress devoted its 1948 Declaration on Human Rights and Obligations to these questions, while the Treaty on Human Rights of 1969 covered the freedom of conscience, religion, thought, and expression.

These precepts opposing mental subjugation and pro-
tecting spiritual values and freedom of religious and intellectual
expression were laid down to prevent legal indoctrination,
and to obstruct religious and emotional coercion. Adam
Doron presents an Israeli view:

> Human history, if it teaches anything at all, teaches
> that first and foremost, any attempt to manipulate
> public or individual religiosity from the upper echelons
> of power must be opposed vigorously by the public.
> It would therefore be a fatal error to assume that
> opposition to religious coercion in Israel would be
> weaker among the Jews than the non-Jews. Moreover,
> those preaching acceptance of uniform Jewish
> religiosity forget that there is no commonly agreed
> standard whatsoever for public spiritual behaviour,
> not even among the Orthodox themselves.[9]

Only a democratic parliamentary regime guided by the
principles of the rule of law, and which has an innate sense
of tolerance, is able to grapple with this onerous task.

Anyone wanting to achieve religious uniformity through
the democratic institutions of the State of Israel impinges
on the rule of law and hence undermines democratic parliamentary structure.

The transition from democratic to totalitarian rule does
not presage the abrogation of the Knesset as a legislative
institution. It is quite adequate for the Knesset itself to impose
precepts on the citizens of Israel in the spheres of faith, philosophy, and lifestyle, and to enforce public observance of religious
ritual. At that point, we will have crossed the Rubicon.

A liberal (by affiliation) and very independent (by political
nomenclature) Knesset member walked out of the plenum
during the debate on the Prohibition of the Sale of Pork

Act, which had been brought solely for purposes of religious ritual.[10] Only 20 percent of the Knesset members used their vote to oppose this law of ritual observance. The very foundation of the rule of law was shattered—and not by an action but by majority vote. Knesset members, who simply voted by rote, washed their hands of the matter, and liberal democracy took another blow.

Between Tolerance and Sufferance

Israeli democracy was definitively outlined in the Declaration of Independence. In the sphere of social equality and integration among Jews and non-Jews it presents monumental problems for Orthodoxy.

Rabbi Yitzhak Peretz is leader of the Shas party and holds the Interior portfolio in the national unity government headed by socialist Shimon Peres. Cabinet Minister Peretz made a polite visit to a Bedouin tribe in the Negev, the semi-desert region of southern Israel. His pronouncements there illustrated all too clearly the ever-widening gap between the Declaration of Independence and the new consensus materializing before us. It is worth quoting Rabbi Peretz directly:

> It is written in the Torah that it is essential for each nation to preserve its character and breed. This is the guarantee for peace among nations. Intermixture leads to hatred, conflict, and war. Since I would like to live in peace, I do not hold with excessively close association between Jewish and Arab youth. At a tender age meetings of this type give rise to love; love leads to marriage. This is neither good nor healthy.[11]

There is nothing new or extreme about Minister Peretz's declaration. To the contrary, it is relatively mild. The novelty lies in announcing publicly, through the media, the halachic stand on relationship with the Gentiles. After all, the halacha forbids even employing a Gentile as a messenger; and it is doubtful whether a Jew may serve food to a Gentile.[12]

The Talmud deals with significant problems for the Jewish people, such as whether, having found something that has been lost, a Jew may return it if he knows the owner is a Gentile. Current view holds that the item should not be returned to a heathen.

Talmud morality categorizes people according to their relationship to the Commandments of Moses. An observing Jew is enjoined to show an especially high moral level to "a colleague of Torah and [observer of the] Commandments." He may be forgiving toward a "criminal" Jew insofar as fulfilling the Commandments, but not to a Gentile, particularly a pagan.[13]

The *Mishneh Torah* of Maimonides (Rambam) deals with the commandments enjoined upon the children of Israel when their entry to the land of Israel coincides with the arrival of the Messiah. Here, their attitude toward the Gentile is specified to the last detail. Regarding non-Jewish women, for example: "A beautiful woman who refuses to stop worshipping idols after twelve months is killed."

The general tenet is that anyone not a member of the people of Israel should be rejected. Even more, "any Gentile not upholding the Noachic commandments is killed if under our rule." The Rambam goes further and determines that all living beings must uphold the Noachic commandments or else be put to death.

The Talmudic Orthodox approach, in fact, does not present leeway for tolerance, while only its milder injunctions display some patience.

Professor Yeshayahu Leibowitz, researcher, historian, and very active philosopher, is well known to the Israeli public. He is something of a maverick in foreign affairs and also a fervent opponent of the religious Orthodox establishment on the issue of separation of religion and state—an issue uniting militant secularists. In his recent book, *On Faith, History, and Values,* Leibowitz devotes an entire chapter to an analysis of tolerance in Orthodox Judaism. He uses Maimonides as his guiding light for one aspect, and the somewhat differently inclined Judges for the other.[14] In analyzing the meaning of tolerance, Leibowitz maintains that it has spiritual rather than judicial stature, but that it also recognizes human rights on a practical level. This clearly puts the evaluation of tolerance in Orthodox Talmudic theology beyond the bounds of the abstract. It has a direct, immediate effect on human rights. This is dangerous for any Orthodox adherent as it poses impossible existentialist questions such as that of freedom of conscience. Can Orthodox theology deal with these problems? Leibowitz answers promptly and sharply. He quotes Maimonides, who demands death for deviants, apostates, and anyone rejecting the Torah as having come from God. It is not, the author emphasizes, a halachic, judicial injunction. "Every man is permitted, and even commanded, to kill them; and no witnesses nor cautioning nor judges are required. Rather, anyone who kills one of them fulfills a great commandment and has removed an impediment."

Rabbi Zvi Moshe Neriah, a former member of the Knesset, and president of Bnei Akiva yeshiva colleges, participated with me in a discussion broadcast on Israel state radio. Said he: "You [as non-Orthodox] can be tolerant; you can be tolerant towards non-kosher eaters, Shabbos-violating Jews, and even mixed marriages. I [as Orthodox] can only be patient."

However, Leibowitz emphasizes that this view of

Maimonides is codified and even specially selected by certain rabbinical judges.

Leibowitz agrees that the gap between religious Orthodox and secular is widening daily, but he puts it in his own way: "Perhaps we will reluctantly arrive at a separation into two nations, with a differentiation not only from the aspect of marriage, but also with each going his historic way imbued by intense hatred [of the other]." If this indeed is the main stand of the Orthodox public in Israel and that of their spiritual leaders, if the religious population truly is convinced that this is the only road to salvation and continued existence for the Jewish people, we are facing an insoluble dispute.

Philosophers are not the only ones who hold this opinion. The topic has caught the attention of a wide range of people. In a 1983 interview with a group of local journalists just before the Jewish New Year, Israel's President Haim Herzog declared:

> The most critical polarization among the Jews in Israel is between the religious and the secular, and even more among the religious themselves. Extremism is taking hold of a specific religious public. In my youth, too, during the British Mandate, there were problems between religious and secular, with the Neturei Karta being the most extreme. But then they were isolated. In my youth there was no extremism and religious fanaticism among those of western origin. In those days I studied at the Hebron Yeshiva . . . almost all the students were members of the Haganah or the Irgun. Today I don't know how many IDF [Israel Defense Forces] soldiers, if any, are to be found in that yeshiva. In the days of my youth the yeshiva's bounds did not reject national underground service.[15]

The constitutional structure of the State of Israel precludes the president from involvement in topics that do not have almost total consensus. He has a minimal practical role in the executive branch. His position is almost wholly symbolic, and his prestige lies solely in the dignity of his post. These constraints make two aspects of President Herzog's statement especially significant: First, the codification of the dispute between religious (Orthodox) and secular; second, the extremism in the religious-Orthodox camp, which prevents the moderating influence of the "liberal" Orthodox.

Moshe Kol, who was a member of various Israeli cabinets for more than a decade, is well versed in his country's political system. He wrote about the aftermath of the Lebanon war, and discussed the situation of soldiers' widows who will experience difficulties due to halachic law if they should want to remarry.[16]

When it comes to rabbinical decisions and halachic law, it is enough to recall a statement made during a radio broadcast by Rabbi Haim Pardess, a member of the Tel Aviv Rabbinical Regional Tribunal:

> Only one thing is the determining factor in my life—Torah and halacha. Aside from that there is no other authority in the world. We have the Torah from Sinai and not from legislators. Suddenly, a new generation has appeared and invented this thing called 'the legislature.' A bunch of clowns sit together at a party and so decide the law. Do you like living with this? Please—live with it. It's none of my business.[17]

The statement evoked wide criticism even before it was published. Rabbi Pardess asked if he could clarify it, but he hadn't the slightest intention of moderating his words. He merely stressed that everything he had said regarding the secular legislators was directed at Knesset laws opposing religious laws, because the only legislation he would accept was that applying to halacha. The views expressed by Rabbi Pardess are not unique. They accurately reflect the attitude of the entire religious establishment as well as the political establishment of the religious parties.

Orthodox intellectuals, whose views in any case are nullified by rabbinical decisions, found no answer to validate the overall sovereignty of the main legislative establishment of the State of Israel. Some of them wanted to give secular rule the status of "takanot ha'kahal" (Jewish community bylaws), and a few brave souls were prepared to accept the principle that the law of the secular Jewish ruler is binding, but only conditionally. If a contradiction should ever arise between the law of the State and religious law, the latter would get preference.

The approach that regards state law as "Gentile" law, and consequently rejects it, concomitantly rejects the national sovereignty of the Jewish people. It glorifies the sovereignty of the rabbis. This point of view is deeply anchored in Talmudic jurisprudence. The Talmudic Encyclopedia quotes from authoritative sources:

> It makes no difference if the case is presented before a Gentile or a Jew, as the substantive law [secular law] is imaginary. The matter is even more disgraceful because the Torah law was exchanged for a vain law [sentence or verdict, the result of secular legislation]. If the people of the community agree with it [the secular law] their agreement is not really valid. If they reject this [reasoning], their jurisdiction is perverted and oppressive and they are striking at the law of Moses.[18]

This view embraces an entire world, with no intention of remaining restricted to the constitutional sphere. One need only recall the manner in which distinguished Orthodox rabbis have presented Western culture. In a broadcast on Israel state radio, for example, Netanya Chief Rabbi Israel Lau pointed out that Judaism gave the Rambam (Maimonides) to humanity and asked, therefore, what Jews were looking for in pop culture. Former Chief Rabbi Shlomo Goren made a historic survey of the disputes between Jewish and Greek cultures, stating, "Two giant cultures clashed in these conflicts: the Jewish culture, which embodies spirituality, supreme goodness, morality, and the world to come; against Hellenism, which stands for power, beauty, hedonism, and effectiveness in this world."[19]

Plato, Aristotle, Greek drama, the scholar-philosophers whose greatness was grounded in the laws of morality, aesthetics, scientific curiosity, cosmography, theology, and more—all were deleted from the glory that was Greece with one stroke of the pen. The associations arising from such a presentation are horrifying. The ordinary person, who is not as intellectual as Rabbis Lau and Goren imagine, might well understand from their august pronouncements that Judaism gave the culture of the Torah to the world while the West desecrates it through rock and roll, punk pop, and materialism.

Elections for the Eleventh Knesset were held on July 23, 1984. Shas, a strictly conformist Orthodox party of Oriental ethnic origin, won four valuable seats. The party joined the national unity government led by Shimon Peres, and its leader holds the Interior portfolio in the Cabinet.

Many of us remember the tragic accident of 1985 in which seventeen Petach Tikva schoolchildren died when their schoolbus collided with a train. The leader of Shas, Rabbi Yitzhak Peretz, went on record that the accident was a punishment from God because of the desecration of the Sabbath in Petach

Tikva.[20] That little town had had the temerity to open movie houses on the Sabbath, evoking violent demonstrations from the Orthodox.

Shas Knesset member Shimon Ben-Shlomo also had his say. At the height of the bloody Lebanon war, he announced that prostitution in the IDF was the reason for our casualties. The Knesset member was making his point against the women soldiers—Orthodox women are exempt from military service.

But these cases were only of minor importance.

With extreme pragmatism, Rabbi Ben-Shlomo publicly declared that he, together with the entire nation of Israel, did not need the Knesset. We have the Torah from Sinai, he said, and we don't need new laws. Extraordinary? No— after all, this is what we were taught by Rabbi Pardess.

The process of invalidating the rule of law is accelerating. Dr. Ya'acov Fogelman, a pious, well-read and approachable American Jew, is prepared to appear before any public group that will give him a hearing. He represents what he calls the Jerusalem Information Centre on Jewish Affairs. He wants to make a completely unambiguous announcement: There is no place for a theocracy in Israel. The expression itself is foreign and creates negative associations. It is invading a different authority, a Torah-cracy, or blue-and-white theocracy.

Past experience has proved that religious legislation filters perfectly well through the parliamentary grid, so it is completely possible to arrive at a Torah-cracy via democracy.

Jerusalem's Nonprofit Organizations Registry lists a nonprofit organization whose purpose is to protect a halachic authority in Israel. The sole statute book of this authority is Talmudic law. Heading this organization is Joel Lerner, who for many years worked with Rabbi Meir Kahane. Lerner also served a prison term imposed by the Jerusalem District Court, which convicted him of establishing an underground gang that had attempted to blow up the Dome of the Rock on the Temple Mount. Various reports[21] indicate that Lerner's new organization won the support of Israel's two chief Orthodox rabbis, Rabbi Mordechai Eliahu and Rabbi Abraham Shapiro. Should the organization achieve its goal and the Torah laws supplant secular, elected Knesset legislation, Knesset member Shimon Ben-Shlomo's wish will unquestionably be fulfilled. It would enable the establishment of the Sanhedrin (the rabbinical tribunal) and Reform Jews would duly be stoned to death for Sabbath desecration.

Rabbi Meir Kahane has won the approval of both Lerner and Knesset member Ben-Shlomo. The latter was asked if he appreciated Kahane's courage. His response: "I value the courage of anyone who says what he believes, and is not afraid of anyone . . . in any event, that is how one should act."[22]

The Jewish Orthodox Church v. Humanism

Rabbi Shlomo Goren, former chief Ashkenazi rabbi of Israel, once said, "Now that extremism has intensified in the religious camp . . . anyone who is craven will be forbidden to enter the synagogue."

Rabbi Richard Hirsch is one of the leaders of religious Reform Jewry in Israel. His movement is the first casualty of extremism in the religious camp. He represents the community to which Professor Yeshayahu Leibowitz even denied religious identity by describing its members as "Jews who remove the yoke of the Torah and Commandments, and [then] regard themselves as 'religious.'"

Thus, Rabbi Hirsch is well aware of the new reality taking shape in Israel right in front of his eyes. He expressed his outlook in a response to a conversation with Rabbi Louis

Bernstein.[23] Rabbi Hirsch may well never have read Leibowitz's book, but the following excerpts from his article neatly outline the thunderous conflict resounding throughout Israel today:

> Rabbi Bernstein and his Orthodox colleagues call for "unity of the Jewish people." But their "unity" carries a price tag marked "uniformity." The unity they demand is on their terms. . . . Conservative and Reform rabbinical leaders have repeatedly expressed a willingness to sit with Orthodox rabbis to negotiate differences within the framework of religion, separated from Israeli politics. But these offers have been consistently rebuffed by the Orthodox with a Khartoum-like formula: No negotiation, no recognition, no peace. . . . They have exercised the political power of the religious parties in Israel's Knesset, and have abused the secular mechanism of the Knesset, composed in the main of secular Jews as well as non-Jewish legislators, to impose halachic standards on the Israeli public. . . .
>
> The Reform and Conservative movements care so deeply about Israel that they refuse to accept second-class status. . . .
>
> The alternative is disinterest and a weakening of the bonds of identity with Israel.

Nevertheless, Rabbi Hirsch comes out very strongly against the moderate religious Orthodox camps, seemingly almost in direct response to former Chief Rabbi Goren in his confession of surrender to the ultra-Orthodox: "The so-called moderate Orthodox leadership represented by the Mizrachi are afraid of the Orthodox right. . . . The moderate Orthodox are being drawn to the right by the ultra-Orthodox and are themselves adopting more militant positions." And here is the heart of the issue, as stated by Rabbi Hirsch: "This has produced an Orthodoxy more intolerant, isolationist, radical, and chauvinistic."

In summary, this means that the principles of the extremist and militant religious Orthodox faith have penetrated the Zionist Orthodox religious camp, which over the years had created for itself an image of moderation. There doubtless are some who will claim that this comes as no surprise. Others will claim that extremism was already embedded in the character of Orthodoxy. This is provided by Rabbi Hirschensohn's life history, his activities, and his institution.[24] Leibowitz's teachings, too, leave no doubt regarding the inclination of the Orthodox camp, both Zionist and non-Zionist.

It must be acknowledged that even today all the constituents of extreme Orthodox ideology cannot be discerned in the overall religious Orthodox public. Very few protest the place of the Hebrew language within Israel's social framework. With its idiomatic raciness and the cultural properties it has evoked, Hebrew remains the language of the people. It is the main means of communication in all spheres, among both Jews and Arabs. The ultra-Orthodox demand that the holy tongue should not be profaned by everyday use, either in speech or in writing, has virtually disappeared. Nevertheless, there is still a lingering echo.

Recounting the events of only one year, 1983, we find the desecration of the graves of the family of Eliezer Ben-Yehuda, the man who resuscitated Hebrew. Although the Zionist religious Orthodox public certainly had no part in this, and unquestionably disapproved of the act, it raised no protest against the hooliganism. Instead, the protest has come from the so-called secularists. The same year saw the repeated spectacle of the national flag being burned by elements strongly suspected of belonging to those anti-Zionist Orthodox groups, isolated from the social mainstream. At the public level, the ultra-Orthodox appear to have suffered a crushing defeat.

Ironically, Agudat Yisrael, the party representing *non-*Zionist Orthodoxy, is successfully invading the area of Israel's rule and its legislative bodies. Agudat Yisrael has representatives in municipal councils all over the country and even plays an active role in the governing coalition of the city hall of Jerusalem. Its chief representative is a deputy mayor with a wide sphere of influence precisely because of his being part of the governmental process. Agudat Yisrael is represented also in the Knesset. Although its strength was strapped by the emergence of Shas on the political scene, as well as the further fission within the religious bloc, the Aguda holds two Knesset seats. Those two members still play a significant role in the power-balance game played by all the religious parties. No government coalition can be achieved without them.

The national unity coalition government has not changed matters in the religious domain. Coalition has not had the effect of outnumbering the religious parties. On the contrary, both coalition leaders, Peres and Shamir, are intensely frightened by the possibility of needing the religious parties in any situation of conflict or misunderstanding—the latter developing at least twice daily between the Labor Alignment and the Likud bloc.

It was largely the ultra-Orthodox, except of course for the extremist Neturei Karta sect, who changed the rules of the game and eliminated the opposition to contacts with the secular Jewish political scene. The tactic worked. The secular system is now forced to deal with a widespread net of Orthodox demands. The current division in the Eleventh Knesset reflects every phase of Orthodox belief. It includes: two representatives from Agudat Yisrael; four from the NRP; one from Tami (The Torah and Tradition Oriental Jewish Movement); four

from Shas (Torah Guardians Oriental Jewish Movement);
two from Morasha (Tradition Movement); one from Kach;
and five from Tehiya (Renaissance Movement), which is close
to Gush Emunim's political aspirations. Only one of Tehiya's
representatives is "religious" in the accepted meaning of the
term, but the party as a whole draws its strength from the
nationalist-religious voters and usually does not find itself
in conflict with Orthodox demand. This is not a homogeneous
bloc, but, as Rabbi Goren himself acknowledged, almost all
the Orthodox groups now follow the extremist line.
Examination of the basic theological approach of these groups
would show that the present leaning toward extremism is
not particularly surprising.

The pioneers of religious cooperation with secular Zionists
were the members of the Mizrachi-NRP movement. Their
achievements were great. First, issues concerning personal
status—marriage and divorce—were transferred exclusively
to the rabbinical judicial system. Second, education in Israel
was divided into three streams, which in turn divided among
themselves the right to influence the souls of future generations.

Each educational stream has its own schools—public-
secular, public-religious (Zionist-Orthodox), and independent
religious (non-Zionist and haredi Orthodox). Every year
contests are held where the souls of the potential students
are the pawns in the game, with the different groups presiding
over the scene. However, the Orthodox groups have managed
to get the best of the deal over their fellow religionists. They
lead in everything—contributions, influence, educational and
rabbinical positions, establishment of norms for rituals such
as kashrut, and service as rabbinical judges in tribunals
throughout the country. Religious Orthodoxy, in all its aspects,
has successfully put an obstacle in front of non-Orthodox
religious Judaism. The political maneuvering has immense

practical implications.

Although the Marriage and Divorce Act of 1953 states that "marriages and divorces in Israel will be performed according to the law of the Torah," the rabbinical tribunals adhere to strict Orthodoxy.[25] They render judgment only on the basis of the most rigid Orthodox tenets, negating any ceremonies held according to other shades of Judaism such as Conservative or Reform. One is left wondering when the diluted Orthodoxy of most western countries will also fall under the axe.

The Chief Rabbinate and local rabbinical and other Jewish religious institutions spring from secular Knesset legislation. Leibowitz's comments on this issue are noteworthy. He observed that the State of Israel is a secular state known outwardly as religious. It falls, he says, within the definition of prostitution of religion. These religious institutions are kept exclusively for representatives of Orthodoxy. To satisfy the Orthodox business public, the State of Israel created a local government system parallel to the one known as a municipal system. In many instances the activities of the religious councils overlap those of the municipal councils, leading to duplication and waste.[26] The religious councils by their own definition are in charge of supplying religious services to Jews who desire to receive them.

Although positions on religious councils nominally should be open to all religious Jews, no Reform or Conservative-affiliated Jew has yet been appointed to them. A test case was brought in an attempt to resolve the matter judicially. The Supreme Court handed down a decision that in principle endorsed the right of non-Orthodox Jews to membership in these bodies, but that is where it remained.[27] Principles of rule of law and Orthodoxy do not mix.

Even more pointed is the discrimination against non-

Orthodox institutions in the distribution of funds. Since all funds for religious affairs remain in the hands of the Orthodox, non-Orthodox Jews stand no chance of receiving what should be their due share.

In Israel, religious theological institutes have the right to receive state-owned land for their buildings. This right has remained very restricted. The Tel Aviv Reform Jews fought a ten-year struggle to win the right to get land for their temple. In Jerusalem, the Conservative Jews have been trying for five years to build a synagogue in the new Ramot neighborhood. Members of the Jerusalem religious council, who are responsible for supplying "religious needs" and who have sole control over the means of doing so, have been in the vanguard of the struggle against allocating land to their Conservative fellow Jews.[28]

It has long been widely known that Reform and Conservative rabbis are not authorized to officiate at ceremonies for their own congregants. They can neither marry, nor divorce, nor bury them. In addition, Reform rabbis are not authorized to serve in their official capacity as chaplains in the Israel Defense Forces. They are not forbidden, however, to join its ranks as fighting soldiers.[29]

During a Knesset debate, the chairman of the State Comptroller's Office revealed that the government allotted billions of shekels to religious-Orthodox organizations following the coalition's agreement. These were to meet the political and sectorial needs of various religious factions represented in the Knesset, even without reasonable criteria regarding the distribution of these public funds.[30] Dialectical reasoning would show that this amount of support in one specific area has a qualitative effect.

Jerusalem Mayor Teddy Kollek has openly opposed the Orthodox extremists, saying that they behave "like the Italian mafia."[31] The late Professor Yigael Yadin, who gained worldwide renown as an archaeologist and later served as deputy prime minister during the first term of the Begin government, described the activities of the ultra-Orthodox as "terror."[32]

The incidence of assault and violence by the Orthodox toward secular and non-Jewish institutions is so high as to have become almost a social norm. Dr. Uzi Ritta, a lecturer at Jerusalem's Hebrew University, was driving one Sabbath in 1983 with his small daughter. Stones were thrown at his car and he was gravely injured. Ritta was hospitalized for a long period with suspected permanent brain damage.

Later, Rabbi Marvin Friedman published a significant statement on this incident, on behalf of what he called the Jewish Moral Committee: "Dr. Uzi Ritta of the Hebrew University is the infamous protagonist of the heretical theories of evolution. In keeping with his theories, he reverted to the primate state by deliberately crashing through the Shabbos Police barriers . . . indeed, it was moral justice!"[33]

A great deal more can be said about the damage to academic freedom due to religious coercion in Israel. At this stage, we will deal with the damage done to the rule of law, and with the gain, according to the Israeli press, accruing to militant Orthodox groups.

As already stated, Ritta's tragedy is not out of the ordinary. It is one of a long list of incidents of religious violence. The *Jerusalem Post* of May 6, 1983, made the following report in an article headed, "'Special' Police Treatment for Ultra-Orthodox": "Police treat ultra-Orthodox groups according to their own discretion, while the rest of Israeli society is handled strictly according to the law, Police Inspector-General Arye Ivtzan said yesterday."[34] This is one illustration of the widespread feeling in Israel that the religious Orthodox have some sort of advantage, and thus an abnormal cultural phenomenon develops and becomes crystallized—the lack of equality between a violator of law who is Orthodox, and one who is a "regular" citizen. When this phenomenon is accompanied by the pressures and violent atmosphere now surrounding religious issues, a new climate results, deviating widely from the specific incident reported by the media.

There is a strong feeling in many sectors of the Israeli public that the next target of militant Orthodoxy will be freedom of scientific research. For the Jewish conscience, ever since its emergence from the provincial ghetto, this freedom has had special significance, while for the Israeli it is even more important. The Israeli is brought up to believe that the special quality of its science, technology, and military has given Israel the advantage over more than 100 million warring Arab neighbors. Israeli agriculture developed in a semi-arid desert environment. Its worldwide renown is largely due to the scientific research carried out at the Volcani and Weizmann Institutes of Science and at the universities and kibbutz institutes. Rational thought and scientific development have always been considered the inalienable dominion of political Zionism and an independent Israel. These elements are also an outstanding attribute of Western culture.

Arnold Toynbee refers to these issues in discussing the advantage the West has held over the East. The problem he attempts to elucidate is just why the West merited this advantage. Toynbee deals with the subject at length in his book *The World and the West*, where he states:

> The secret of the West's superiority to the rest of the world in the art of war from the seventeenth century onwards is not to be found just in Western weapons, drill and military training. It is not even to be found

just in the civilian technology that supplies the military equipment. It cannot be understood without also taking into account the whole mind and soul of the Western society of the day: and the truth is that the Western art of war has always been one fact of the Western way of life.[35]

Its very nature puts Orthodox halacha at odds with the Western world. Its pride is the prevention of Hellenism. The clash with Western culture, the isolation that verges on xenophobia, the attitude of "they hate us"—these are all manifestations of avoiding Hellenization. Some Orthodox even oppose sports, a direct symbol of that ancient fear of the Greek. One has only to recall the attack waged and won by Jerusalem's Orthodox militants against the construction of a soccer field and swimming pools in the city. Many groups in Orthodox Judaism despise sports as an expression of debasement before an alien culture. More moderate Orthodox groups indeed have been drawn into the modern enthusiasm and have established their own sports associations, training and performing on weekdays only. But even there we see evidence of increasing extremism. Time will tell what the final direction will be.

The defense used by the Orthodox is that it is precisely this isolation and segregation that have preserved the nation of Israel for 2,000 years of dispersion and that have prevented assimilation.

Aluf Har-Even, of Jerusalem's Van Leer Institute, wrote as follows against this conservatism:

The ability to exist as a nation for over 100 generations does not mean that the Jews could exist forever without altering those lifestyles and those political frameworks. In a cruel way, we can say that the Jewish lifestyle that collapsed was that belonging to its founders, who did not have sufficient insight to find new solutions to problems of a changing reality, and, alternately, on those occasions when the Jews did succeed in finding a different lifestyle by adapting to a changing reality, they also found they were able to continue their Jewish existence.[36]

An Israel that refused to merge with a Western culture based on the political Zionist heritage and on scientific research to which the Jews had made such an immense contribution; an Israel that put mysticism before rationalism, theological uniformity and conformity before pluralism; this Israel would be put to a test that it would probably fail.

The struggle in Israel for freedom of research has reached a peak. Ironically, the most violent of the conflicts between the disciples of science and the guardians of Orthodox halacha have concerned the freedom to carry out archaeological research.

In 1983, the Israeli media swelled with descriptions of demonstrations by religious extremists, but the reason for them was almost forgotten. The reason was Dr. Yigal Shiloh of Jerusalem's Hebrew University, who was leading the dig at the City of David site. The excavation had already produced remarkable artifacts dating from the reign of the shepherd-turned-king, and the academic world was agog.

Not so the religious Orthodox. They claimed that the site is an ancient Jewish cemetery, and hence it is forbidden to dig there. Archaeologists maintained that the claim about a cemetery was unfounded. Then-Chief Rabbi Shlomo Goren came roaring into the lists. Rabbi Goren is a Zionist regarded as a "moderate" Orthodox. He publicly attempted to justify the claim of the religious extremists. The charge of the Orthodox boiled down to the assertion that if there indeed was uncertainty about the nature of the site, the religious authorities should have the final say on whether the excavations should continue.[37]

Dr. Shiloh already had a valid permit to carry out the dig, so well-organized demonstrations were begun by the Orthodox militants. They brandished placards bearing a macabre legend that equated the Holocaust with the excavations: "1938 in Europe, 1983 on the Temple Mount in Jerusalem."[38] The extremist Orthodox groups, supported as they were by some leaders of the Zionist religious-Orthodox establishment, gathered strength. The demonstrations became violent and sometimes bloody conflicts. The irony already inherent in the situation was enhanced. These people, after all, were battling because of their burning desire to protect the holiness of what they maintained were ancient cemeteries. Yet they did not hesitate to desecrate a modern gravesite, that of one of the great archaeologists of Israel, Professor Sukenik, father of Professor Yigael Yadin, also renowned in the same field. It was then that Professor Yadin characterized these acts as terrorism, and the mayor of Jerusalem accused the perpetrators of using Mafia-like methods.

To show the feeling prevalent in Jerusalem at the time, here is a description by an Israeli journalist:

> It was at the end of the season of demonstrations because it was the end of the season of excavations at Area 'G.' Yigal Shilo, director of the City of David excavations which include Area 'G,' was at the demonstrations too.
>
> Shilo, arch-enemy of Edah haredit, said he was there just in case things got out of hand and the

haredim moved into his office, less than 100 meters from the demonstration site.

It was hard to see what he could have done against a crowd of over 6,000, but while he was there he had a few vociferous arguments with some members of the Edah, whom he has come to know from all those years of conflict with them.[39]

The violent demonstrations at the dig, the conflict between the scientists and the religious masses, all served as a backdrop for a constitutional struggle that was taking place simultaneously in the Knesset. The real focus of the drama was here. Knesset members representing Agudat Yisrael declared they would walk out of Begin's precariously balanced coalition government if a law to preserve cemeteries was not enacted. That piece of legislation eventually became popularly known as the Archaeology Law. If the ultimatum were carried out it would mean the fall of the Likud government.

While the Labor opposition predictably opposed the bill, there was unexpected and strong opposition to it from parties supporting the government—the Liberals being particularly surprising in their condemnation. The bill slipped through its final reading in a piece of neat parliamentary chicanery.

But that wasn't the end of the drama. The following day, the Knesset speaker announced that the bill had been passed in violation of the regulations of the Knesset, when most of the members were absent and when the reading had not even been featured on the Knesset agenda. Opinion was divided about the so-called unparliamentary action, and the dispute continued.[40]

The steamroller tactics of the Orthodox are effective because eventually their votes are needed to prop up a tottering coalition government. No Israeli government has been viable without their support.

The case of the archaeologists' struggle for academic freedom to investigate Israel's past is not unique. It is part of a long series of conflicts leading to the Kulturkampf actually taking place today.

In March 1983 the First Congress on Investigation into the Origin of Life and Evolution was held at the Truman Institute on the Hebrew University's Mount Scopus campus in Jerusalem. It took place under the auspices of the Ministry of Culture and Education, at that time headed by Zevulun Hammer, a member of the NRP. The conference was regarded as particularly prestigious because it was supported by the National Council for Research and Development as well as the Israel Academy of Sciences. The opening day of the conference revealed a sharp division among the participants, some of whom claimed the conference was rigged, giving the limelight to the fundamentalist creationists as opposed to the evolutionists. A serious scientific conference faced the challenge of whether it is possible to bridge the gap between the religious-Orthodox Jewish point of view and the theory of evolution.

Professor Ephraim Urbach, who on his own claim is religious and who is president of the Academy of Sciences, made some harsh accusations in his opening speech. He claimed that an antiscientific atmosphere had been created around the conference. Rhetorically, he asked whether an antiscientific conference could possibly be supported. Continuing, he said that in Israel, as well as throughout the rest of the world, a fundamentalist approach was developing. The essence of fundamentalism was that nothing was important that was not mentioned in the Torah, or the Bible, or the Koran. This approach, he added, was spreading among the religious groups of Israel. As a man who had faith, he felt that this fundamentalist approach added nothing to the power of religious belief. Just the opposite, in fact—the scientific approach cannot harm faith.

In Urbach's opinion, religion is not science, nor does it even try to be science. It is doubtful if his opinion will be accepted by those speaking in the name of Orthodoxy. However, the very fact that he expressed it emphasizes the Kulturkampf in Israel.[41]

This conflict stretches across a wide front. In June 1983, the Utah Oratorio Choir, a Mormon group who were members of the Mormon Utah Oratorio Society, visited Jerusalem. The Mormon singers' program included Handel's *Messiah*, and they were to perform at the impressive hall of Binyanei Ha'umah. On the night of June 9, before the concert began, about one hundred yeshiva students from the Mercaz Ha'Rav yeshiva, affiliated with the Zionist nationalist Orthodox stream, demonstrated outside the hall. When the oratorio was already under way about fifteen students who had bought tickets and were seated in the hall rushed down the aisles and leaped on the stage, shouting slogans as they tore down the national flag. Members of the audience grappled with the demonstrators and hustled them out. The yeshiva students managed to disrupt the concert, but not to stop it.[42]

It was learned afterward that Ashkenazi Chief Rabbi Avraham Shapiro had sanctioned a nonviolent demonstration. He told the students, who asked if they were halachically permitted to demonstrate against the concert, that they could not remain silent about it. Rabbi Yigal Safran, assistant to the Chief Rabbi, told the press that the real objection was the use of the hall. The Binyanei Ha'Umah belongs to the Jewish Agency, and it was felt inappropriate that the *Messiah* should be performed there.

When Rabbi Meir Kahane held his party convention in

Binyanei Ha'umah on February 12, 1986, the same Orthodox establishment, so sensitive about the Mormon choir, was completely silent about the appropriateness of the Jewish Defense League calling for a Jewish state "clean" of Gentiles.

The Orthodox establishment was also distressed about the Mormons' performance of the *Messiah*, because the libretto had been distributed to the audience. It would all have been quite acceptable, said Rabbi Safran, if the Mormon choir had performed the *Messiah* at the Catholic abbey of Abu Ghosh. In fact, they pressed the organizers to hold the concert in Abu Ghosh, where the Mormon singers had previously performed.

Then, the religious Orthodox had no objections whatsoever against the Mormons; they objected only to the *Messiah*, and that merely because it was sung in a particular hall, and because the libretto was distributed. Today, they object to the *Messiah* sung anywhere. Today, they also object to the Mormons.

At the time I didn't hesitate to protest. I said that I didn't intend going into the students' behavior. The essence of my comments was that the public had suddenly learned that the struggle against universal cultural values doesn't belong only to the members of the Neturei Karta or the followers of the Szatmar rabbi. For some unknown reason it had long been hidden from us that religious Orthodoxy, both anti-Zionist as well as messianic Zionist, is struggling not only against desecration of the Sabbath but also against the values of tolerance.

Today, with the recruiting of yeshiva students in the struggle against a master composer and a creation that is a mark of Western cultural achievement, and against a Gentile choir, it has been proved that we are in the midst of a Kulturkampf of the worst order. It is a war whose victory will end in religious and cultural isolation, hatred of foreigners, dissociation from Western culture, and, whatever else happens, contraction into the confines of a lifestyle that contradicts everything that the original Zionists foresaw.

A parochial vision of an autonomous ghetto stalks the land.

After only two years the Kulturkampf took on another threatening dimension. This time Mormon academic activities were the focus of the struggle. Since 1970 an extension of the Mormon Brigham Young University has functioned in Jerusalem. For years classes were held without disturbance in rented premises at Kibbutz Ramat Rachel on the southwestern border of Jerusalem. In 1983 the university bought a plot of land on Mount Scopus with the intention of building its own campus. University officials presented blueprints for authorization to the two statutory committees whose approval was required. They had the approval of the Council for Higher Education, of the Minister of Education and Culture, and of the local as well as district statutory planning bodies. They also had the formal approval of the Ministry of Foreign Affairs, this last being required because the Brigham Young University officials are Americans. The project was approved, licensed, stamped, and blessed. Construction of the building began, and it was already at three-story height by late 1984. Still all was quiet.

Then the storm broke, although by no means spontaneously. Rather, it was completely and deliberately orchestrated. The religious groups opened the attack. They were headed by Yad L'Achim, a non-Zionist, so-called anti-missionary organization with haredi leanings. Looking back at the demonstration two and a half years earlier against the Mormon performance of the *Messiah,* one saw the protests as total lunacy. But lunatics are dangerous. This attack on the

Mormons isn't a one-time, or even seasonal, demonstration. It is total war.

The head of the Jerusalem extension of Brigham Young University, who lives permanently in Jerusalem, appeared on Israel TV and ran a tape of the threats he and other associates had received. The recording contained expressions that were frighteningly familiar to Jews: "Dirty Christian! Get out of here! Go back to America! If you don't stop that building [the Jerusalem campus] we'll kidnap your children and burn your cars."

The religious groups claim that by the tenets of their faith the Mormons are commanded to proselytize, and of course the Jews won't accept this. Another claim is that the location of another university so close to the Hebrew University on Mount Scopus is likewise unacceptable because it endangers the tender susceptibilities of Jewish students and lecturers. It is additionally provocative because it overlooks the Temple Mount. But rather than the location of the Mormon University, its very existence is the real problem, precisely in the same way the existence of the Jew distresses the anti-Semite.

We cannot ignore, however, the claim that a good Mormon is one who carries out his missionary command. All the monotheistic religions, after all, are dedicated to that premise. Islam enjoins that this command be carried out even by violence—the "jihad," or holy war. Since its inception, Christianity in all its denominations has dabbled in missionary activity. The Spanish Inquisition and the events that took place throughout Europe and South America indicate that even Christianity did not abhor violence when it came to increasing the number of believers.

Indeed, it was precisely because of its awareness of this that the Israeli legislature passed a special directive in its penal code that prohibits the offering of compensation as a reward for conversion.[43] There is not much other scope for Christian missionary activity in Israel. Paradoxically, the Jewish religious Orthodox establishment is widely involved with proselytizing among non-Orthodox Jews, and it is time to extend the directives of the law prohibiting enticement for purposes of religious conversion to the repentance ("hazara b'teshuva") activities as well.[44]

The Orthodox campaign against the Mormons has become institutionalized. In December 1984, Agudat Yisrael proposed a motion of no confidence in the government because of its refusal to stop the construction of the Mormon university. The other religious parties pressured the government into establishing a special cabinet committee to investigate attitudes about the construction of the university. We should not take this injunction against the Mormon university too lightly. The very establishment of a cabinet committee implies that the Mormons should be investigated, and that their activities will be investigated in a manner to which the academic and religious activities of Jews—at least the Orthodox ones—are not subjected. If the responsible authorities of the Mormon university extension do not comply with Israeli law, it is a matter not for a cabinet committee but for the police to investigate the situation and to prosecute the accused for breaking the law. And if the university authorities are found innocent, what will a committee of the Israeli cabinet do?

It is not the Mormons who were harmed by the government decision. World opinion questioned the rule of law in Israel and the image of Israel as a democratic, pluralistic state that enshrines freedom of religion, science, and conscience.[45]

The Chief Orthodox Rabbinate, which in my opinion is a kind of Jewish Episcopal Church pretending to represent world Judaism, convened an extraordinary meeting and decided on a "Sabbath of outcry and protest" throughout the Jewish world. Orthodox Jews thus initiated a worldwide conflict with the Christian Mormons. It is apparently comfortable to attack the Mormons. They are not happily accepted by their fellow Christians and, like the Jews, they are a persecuted minority.

But one should not believe that Jewish Orthodoxy hates only the Mormons. The Mormons, after all, were not among the inquisitors nor are they the ones who sanctioned pogroms. The orchestrated campaign against the Mormons is a warning to all non-Jewish religious beliefs in Israel. A generation of religious Jews has now arisen that is imbued with the conviction that it must participate in holy wars like the Christian Crusades and the Moslem jihad. Once again Orthodox Judaism is standing firm in challenge against the outside world.

This approach emphasizes only one aspect, although a significant one, of a wider struggle conducted by Orthodox Judaism against the Gentiles and against conflicting lines of thought within the religious Jewish community.

It is sufficient to recall the deliberate campaign instigated in 1956 against the establishment of the prestigious Hebrew Union College, an extension of Reform Judaism. Then-Chief Sephardic Rabbi Yitzhak Nissim had a dramatic call: "Let us not forget what Reform Judaism did to the people of Israel. It propagated assimilation and absorption in the Diaspora; it erased the memory of Jerusalem from books of prayer; and it blunted all Jewish and national awareness." However, Rabbi Nissim had to deal with the facts of life. Reform Judaism, after all, had adherents who wanted to build their homes in Jerusalem and who played key roles in the Zionist movement. Here is his response: "And if the leaders of this movement should also be appointed among the protagonists for the State of Israel, this should not be regarded as a return to Judaism."[46]

On August 12, 1956, then-mayor of Jerusalem, Gershon Agron, spoke movingly in praise of the archaeology school established by Hebrew Union College and the Reform movement, but the campaign of the Orthodox groups intensified, and incidents were reported.[47] In any event, the construction of the institute was completed, and today it stands on the brink of impressive expansion; but the conflict between Orthodox and Reform Jews is expanding too.

Which Are the Most Chosen People?

The atrocities of the Orthodox "religious Cossacks"[48] against the Christians have, so far, been left to the febrile imagination of the religious Orthodox at grassroots level. The persecution of the Reform Jews isn't organized in the upper echelons either. But the Orthodox rabbinical establishment and the religious political parties directly and deliberately orchestrate the long-term actions—questioning the legitimacy of activities, inflicting public humiliation, stigmatizing the Reform Jews as deviants and a threat to the survival of Judaism.

The Chief Rabbinate in Jerusalem, acting as a statutory body, annually publishes formal declarations warning worshippers that High Holiday prayers are not acceptable to our God, Lord of the Universe, if they are offered within the confines of Reform and Conservative houses of prayer.

Reform and Conservative communities are denied their rightful share of the financial cake at every level—state government, local authorities, and religious councils. Formal Knesset legislation also puts Reform and Conservative Jews, as individuals, beyond the pale.

The law prohibiting fraud in the dietary (kashrut) laws, which ostensibly was intended to prevent the public being misled on any matter dealing with the sale of goods carrying the "kosher" label, sounds noble but is as fraudulent as the deceit it aims to prevent.[49] In practice, it is merely a useful fiction enabling the Orthodox Rabbinate to monopolize all aspects of awarding the coveted kashrut certificate. This monopoly should not be underestimated; it embraces powerful economic interests. The only persons or organizations that have the right to authorize kashrut certificates are the Chief Rabbinical Council, or a rabbi ordained by that council, or a local rabbi who also is under the aegis of the Chief Rabbinate. The monopoly also encompasses the needs of the Israel Defense Forces (IDF).

Not sharing the monopoly is the ultra-Orthodox (haredi) rabbinate, which operates under the aegis of the Council of Torah Sages and the private "Justice Tribunal" of the haredi community. Haredi rabbis, whose skill and reliability in ritual dietary rules are undeniable, do not enjoy their authority by virtue of the law of kashrut but only by the good graces of the competitive and monopolistic Chief Rabbinate.

This maneuver effectively prevents the Conservative community from issuing its own certificates of kashrut. It also deprives the Conservatives of the large income quietly derived from the issue of the certificates.

Reform and Conservative rabbis are not only forbidden to officiate in the IDF but also, because the IDF Chief Rabbi is always Orthodox, they are denied official recognition of the sanctity of their calling.

Synagogues in public places, such as airports, hospitals, and universities, and even the Knesset building, are restricted to Orthodox ritual. Non-Orthodox Jewish services where men and women pray together are not permitted to be held in them. That is by no means the only example of discrimination against non-Orthodox Jews; discrimination is also found in education and with regard to personal status.

These examples demonstrate the ambivalence surrounding the rule of law in Israel. They show how a democratic polity has capitulated and surrendered the rule of law in the most vital spheres of life.

When the United Nations adopted the Universal Declaration of Human Rights in 1948, it was regarded as constituting an integral part of the legal system of all member nations. The State of Israel tacitly acknowledged this when it joined the United Nations. The declaration is not simply a broad statement; Articles 18 and 19 are very explicit about freedom of thought, conscience, and religion. Nevertheless, the declaration has no binding power because it is not a formal treaty that requires ratification. However, the International Treaty of Civil and Political Rights of 1966 not only deals specifically with freedom of religion but also obliges any signatory to actively permit freedom of religion in education, in ritual, and in outward expressions of faith. Israel did not sign the treaty then, and twenty years later there is still no indication that it will do so.

The only U.N. treaty accepted by Israel as legally binding was the international treaty against all forms of racial discrimination.[50] Israel, as the state of a people persecuted solely because of their religion and race, could scarcely refuse to sign the treaty. Indeed, it strictly fulfills the command of presenting an annual report to the United Nations concerning compliance. Article 5 of this treaty obliges the signatory not only to refrain from racial discrimination but also to ensure equality before the law regardless of race, nationality, and creed. In brief, by signing this treaty Israel is committed to refrain from moral oppression and obliged to ensure freedom of conscience and religion.

This treaty appears to acknowledge the legality of Israel's own Declaration of Independence. It appears to be another expression of the biblical statement, "and God created man in His own image."[51] It appears to follow the teaching of Rabbi Akiba to "Love thy neighbor as thou wouldst love thine own self."[52] It appears that the provisions of the treaty conform to halachic sources that endow mankind with the constitutional power to reject other laws. Humanistic declarations in Talmudic halacha are, in fact, minimal. The Talmud explains that this power is acknowledged more to prevent hatred than to encourage peace.[53] In other words, the halacha agreed to honor humanity for its own sake, even if Gentile, not because of principles of equality but simply for a pragmatic reason: it was necessary.[54]

Polls showed that the increasing political strength of Rabbi Meir Kahane might even enable him to gain support from the religious and right-wing parties. This created an extremely pragmatic consensus, and the Knesset promptly voted an amendment to the "Basic Law: The Knesset."[55] The amendment essentially states that any faction with a platform constituting racial incitement is forbidden to participate in elections for the Knesset.

There is nothing in this amendment actually to prevent racial incitement. That is not its purpose. It merely prevents a political faction that successfully instigates racial tensions from running for Knesset membership. It is interesting to note that there is no parallel prohibition against a racist faction's participation in municipal elections.

In 1985, an amendment to the penal code was proposed. The purpose was to strengthen the penal code by prohibition of racial incitement. When the government tabled the bill on April 17, 1985, it was found to contain a comprehensive, specific definition of racism—persecution, degradation, or humiliation of the public, or any part of the public; or causing friction between different population groups; or hostility and violence in the framework of race, nationality, or religion.

Had the bill been passed, as suggested in the blueprint, a number of events would have come within the scope of its definition of racism: the statement by then-Chief Rabbi Yitzhak Nissim condemning Reform Judaism; the continuously renewed bans on non-Orthodox Judaism; and the plotting against, negative publicity about, and verbal attacks on the Mormon community because of its legitimate construction of a university extension in Jerusalem. Because the scope of the amendment was so wide, all these issues could have been defined as racism.

If the bill had been passed in the Knesset without substantial changes it would, at the very least, have been proof of the State of Israel's adherence to the international treaty concerning racism. This amendment does not forbid racism as such, nor does it forbid incitement to racism perpetrated by members of the Knesset protected by their parliamentary immunity. But even this limited amendment was not accepted.

One year and more after the Israeli government submitted the racism bill, the Knesset passed into law a diluted version of the bill, only after the Labor Party Alignment agreed to the Likud condition to ban unauthorized contacts between Israeli citizens and leaders of the Palestine Liberation Organization (PLO). Rabbi Meir Kahane, against whom the original bill was conceived, voted in favor of the diluted version along with National Religious Party representatives and almost all coalition members. Ironically, abstentions were cast by Shas, Agudat Yisrael, and Gush Emunim supporting

Tehiya members of the Knesset.

The solution, which satisfied the supporters of the compromise, pertained to two points: First, the bill now requires intent to incite to racism. This phrase, imposing a heavy burden of proof on the prosecution, is one of the main elements that watered down the racism law relative to its draft proposal. Second, the law protects the publication of something that "aims at preserving the character, uniqueness or worship of a religion, provided that this was not done with the object of inciting to racism."[56] This change excludes from the law's scope the publication of matter that aims to preserve the character or uniqueness of a religion. It involves also the case of a person in possession of racist material meant for distribution.

While discussing this bill the past president of the (Conservative) Rabbinical Assembly stated: "Is halacha racist? The answer depends on halacha according to whom? According to the Orthodox religious bloc in the Knesset and the Chief Rabbinate, halacha is racist. Otherwise, how would we explain the amendment put forward by the former to include a clause in the proposed anti-racist bill specifically exempting halacha from the provisions of the law?"[57]

Jewish Horizons of the State

In his capacity as prime minister of Israel and head of the Labor Party, Shimon Peres declared that the preservation of the Sabbath is a national principle and not a coalition topic.[58] As a result of this statement, we may mistakenly draw the conclusion that the socialist leader, as part of his "national heritage," accepts the Torah's capital punishment prescription for desecrations of the Sabbath along with fourteen other crimes, such as murder, adultery, homosexuality, etc., which, as a matter of principle, were subject to capital punishment as well. The socialist-liberal leader hence identified with what was for him a somewhat uncharacteristic approach. This approach holds that, rather than the people of Israel preserving the Sabbath, the Sabbath preserved the people. So possibly Peres agrees with the attitude of the Chabbad followers of the Lubavitcher Rabbi, who pasted on their "mitzvah tank" the motto, "Guard the mezuzah and the mezuzah will guard you."

Actually, the problem is more complicated and rather more serious than could have been anticipated from the long-term point of view, which is not part of political tactics. The real issue is the way of life in Israel, and an investigation into just how far it is possible to realize Zionism and to build a creative, receptive, and open society by determining ritual restrictions and categories for the day-to-day life of the average person.[59]

No one disagrees about the importance of agriculture in Israel, nor about the significance of the agrarian framework that enabled the wandering and exiled Jew to return and take hold of the land. The Moshav Ovdim (collective farm) is one of the distinguished signs of the revolution brought about by the people of Israel in their country. And precisely because agrarian life has implications far beyond the economic level, it too is a target for conflicts between the religious Orthodox and the secular population. Owing to the incentives poured into organized agriculture by both the government and the Israel Lands Authority, the Israeli farmer is caught in the pincers of the political establishment. His dependence on the establishment draws agriculture, too, into the web of party politics. And here, too, the religious parties undoubtedly will establish their hegemony.

Since the mid-sixties, the religious factions have insisted that the moshavim, or collective farms, that are within their political and theological sphere retain this association through successive generations. There was a demand for articles of association that would determine the religious way of life for each moshav. The terms of these articles would be a sine qua non both for membership and for the transfer of land ownership from father to son.

Those terms covered the minutest details of daily living. The Sabbath would have to be observed strictly according to Orthodox ritual—no traveling, and so no family visits; no Friday-night television; regular attendance at the synagogue; and strict observance by married women of the rules of ritual bathing. It was a long list, and any digression whatsoever from Orthodox ritual would mean that the farmer could be thrown off the land. If the son of the family were found to be breaking any of the rules, he would forfeit his patrimony.

The religious parties insisted that all these completely unconstitutional conditions be firmly anchored in law. The moshavim, however, were long since established according to the melting-pot pattern of the Yishuv and later the State, and the pattern was not easily broken. In any event, the bill never got very far, but it was an ominous warning of the determination in the Orthodox camp.[60]

Prime Minister Peres's statement giving legitimacy to the Orthodox Sabbath should be understood in conjunction with the attempted takeover of the moshav lifestyle.

The same goes for the "Shabbes goy," the Gentile who replaces the Jew on the Sabbath and by whose work the Orthodox Jew celebrates the pleasures of the Sabbath. The very essence of Zionism as a Jewish movement of national liberation was not only to have the Jews return to their ancient fatherland and native language, but also to end their dependence on the Gentile neighborhood. It was a Zionist vision to have Jewish farmers and Jewish workers, rather than only Jewish merchants depending on Gentile supply. The religious-Orthodox restriction that prevents Jews from working on the Sabbath; that authorizes rabbis to issue special permits for Jews exercising certain life saving activities on the Sabbath; and replaces Jews by Gentiles on the Sabbath, contradicts this essential Zionist tenet.

In real terms, the conflict over the character of a weekly day of rest in Israel is no longer a struggle for the comfort of the majority who want to make the most ·of that one free day. Rather, this is a titanic struggle surrounding the lifestyle and rights of anyone living in Israel. It will also decide whether Jews in Israel are a self-sufficient nation or a dependent, ghetto-like community.

While leaders like Shimon Peres represent what is known in Israel as "secular Orthodoxy," there are many Israelis who are completely secular but who retain a kind of umbilical cord to an Orthodox past. Professor Shlomo Avineri defined them as Jews who are not attached to any religious community and who do not worship God in any formal way, but the synagogue with which they are affiliated—although they never enter it—is unquestionably Orthodox. Since the real struggle concerns the Jewish and humanistic horizons of the state of the Jews, Israel is meanwhile paying a high price for such ambivalence.

We are confronted with two goals on a collision course—the Zionist aim of establishing a state for Jews that would be completely self-sufficient, and the conflicting Orthodox aim of establishing a lifestyle that will forever necessitate total dependence on non-Jews once a week. Or do the Orthodox envisage a situation where part of the Jewish population remains permanently second-class and not quite kosher?

Once again we see a confrontation between the sovereign state and the isolated community that crystallized in the Diaspora and whose values are now being transferred to an ill-fitting Israeli reality.

When the State of Israel was established in 1948, the Declaration of Independence was its guiding light. It gave unfettered expression to the liberal, enlightened aims of a government that, by the essence of this declaration, was secular and democratic. It seemed then that the suspicions of Rabbi Hirschensohn, decades earlier, had been realized—the state received its independence as a democratic entity, drawing freely, and to our misfortune, on a hodge-podge heritage. That heritage included the British, from whom we obtained the very structure of the government; the French, for the separation of central authorities; the American, for the concept of government of, by, and for the people; and finally the cultural heritage of humanistic Judaism. The founding fathers, led by David Ben-Gurion, were clearly aware of a basic fact—democratic rule requires pluralism and equality.

Israel is composed of various ethnic groups that have immigrated during the past century. They came from Asia as well as Eastern Europe. There is also a significant minority of non-Jewish communities, mainly Moslem and Christian Arabs but also Druze, Armenians, and Bahais. Such a collection of castes, classes, denominations, beliefs, entities, cultures, and heritages can easily became a tinderbox of violence. One need only consider Cyprus and Lebanon.

A carefully balanced democratic system, seriously committed to pluralism and freedom of belief and culture, is the only system able to relieve the tensions and antagonisms the troubled Israeli political entity is facing. Deviations from such a system will result in strengthening the negative forces in

Israeli society. Despite its obvious flaws, it is important to stress some of the tremendous and continuing successes of Israeli democracy: *judicial impartiality*—democratic elections and democratic transfer of power, which have been exercised in the best constitutional tradition; *freedom of speech*—untouched, in spite of a permanent state of war with neighboring countries for thirty-eight years; *appreciation of the respect for parliamentary institutions*—although an erosion of this attitude is unfortunately becoming evident.

Nevertheless, it must be admitted that the future of Israeli democracy is unpredictable. A wide range of reasons leads to this conclusion, but the following are among the most significant and obvious: traditional reliance on mystical beliefs; interpretations of the Talmud by certain ultra-Orthodox sects that reject the Jewish state as an evil institution; the new religious-nationalistic attitude toward the "rabbinical democracy" and toward the disputed territories of Judea and Samaria; and discrimination against non-Orthodox Jewish denominations. These political differences contain ideological and theological dynamite and undermine rational and reasonable persuasion.

A further exacerbation of tensions comes from the fact that the Orthodox establishment has succeeded in avoiding a written constitution, believing that the holy Torah was, and still is, the only constitution the Jewish state needs. As a result, there has been no nationally accepted constitutional common denominator. The confusion inherent in such a vacuum is growing, and the gap between religious heritage and the Western pattern is deepening. The British constitutional framework is still accepted by the legislature and by the courts. On the other hand, the Jewish tradition, which includes a wide range of behavioral rituals, has a strong influence.

Jews collectively have a deeply traditional, common

national conscience, atavistic in nature. It believes that Jewish glory has always been derived from the Torah, in contradiction to Hellenistic influence. The question arises: Will the State of Israel be able to preserve its sovereignty if it loses its democratic, liberal, and pluralistic standards of behavior? Moreover, if Israel becomes a uniformly clerical state, totally absorbed in theological aims, would it be able to preserve cultural ties and connections based on brotherhood and understanding with the entire Western world?

It is an unavoidable conclusion that if the state of affairs in Israel today is allowed to continue, a totally nonpluralistic environment will develop. This development is not irreversible, but only a result of the indifference that has existed and remains a continuing factor. It is unfortunate that instead of under-standing the erosion that affects the future of the unstable constitutional system, those who could help change matters are inactive and have been content with "pragmatic solutions" that have led nowhere. Should this clerical isolationism and xenophobia continue, the result will be a state lacking a democratic structure.

If this is the trend, a pro-Western political orientation will cease to be a sine qua non for Israeli policymakers. Any alliance with the West, even if reached temporarily, would no longer express the cultural and intellectual ties that have previously been significant.

Superficially, there is nothing bad about ancient roots. But any rational thought acknowledges that behind the claim of returning to cultural sources lurks the real aim of enforcing the intolerant Orthodox interpretation of the Torah. This ap-proach evoked tough criticism from non-establishment Or-thodox groups, and from people like Dr. Alice Shalvi of Jerusalem's Hebrew University, and the dean of Bar Ilan University, Professor Rockman.

This crossed, or "clashed," culture is something I call *Casstel.* This portmanteau word expresses the two constituents that sprang from Western culture: the *casbah,* in which the North African Jews lived, and the *shtetl* of the Jews of Eastern Europe.

Professor A. Levontin[61] claims that Jewish atavism has increased because we were not able to form a secular Israeli culture. He maintains that Zionism no longer is the Jewish people's struggle for its normalization, but rather a way of preserving Judaism according to the traditional recipe but with new constituents:

> We read in the press recently that the Tax Authority asked the chief rabbis whether not reporting an income or tax evasion is not forbidden according to the halacha. Apparently it is not good enough if specific behavior is a transgression of the rule of law. It seems that against the backdrop of Jewish history, the rules of law are merely episodes, so there is no real transgression. . . . [If] a state attempts to legitimate laws that originate outside the democratic process . . . how far can it honor the process, [or] its laws, [or] itself?

Here again, as in the case of the skin bank, we see the theological and clerical-religious influence on subjects considered unconditionally secular and theoretically under secular jurisdiction. Nonetheless, the skin bank so vital to saving lives was closed for three years. It was only possible to reopen it after authorization was granted on terms laid down by the Chief Rabbis.[62]

Professor Levontin suspects that the essence of Jewish theology is about to smash our path toward Western-style rule for a long time. He is not the only one who feels that to ensure liberal-democratic rule it is essential to separate religion and state and that it is doubtful that it will be possible to do so because of the religious Jewish approach, which draws on Jewish history where the people of Israel and the religion of Israel are one and the same.

This is the true source of the apparent ambivalence.[63] Without the separation—and there is virtually no chance of it—the law of the Torah according to religious-Orthodox interpretation will be forced on the entire people. The process is at its apogee; there is no room for compromise.

Already every Israeli is dependent on the Orthodox religious ritual from birth through marriage to death and burial. Nevertheless, it would be unwise to claim that it is possible to maintain a human society without religion. But granting equal rights in Israel to all currents in the Jewish faith is not only a moral necessity of an established society; it is the only way to prevent a dictatorship by one of them.

Were the attempt to succeed, the State of Israel would be blessed with freedom of religious ritual, which in turn would strengthen pluralistic rule. A secular democracy could then survive, as the non-Orthodox currents of religious Judaism emphasize the personal and emotional experience. In addition, they contain the essential constituents that formed the relationship between religion and state in Western civilization—a relationship that gave birth to secular and pluralistic democracy.

This is why non-Orthodox Jews must exercise all their influence to disassemble the Orthodox monopoly over religious life in Israel. This is why the balance of power between the various religious Jewish creeds is so essential, not only because of the theological questions involved but also because of the related political attitudes.

No society in the world has been successful in eliminating

a belief in God. For this reason, the interpretation of God in any society is a crucial question. A non-Orthodox and nonchauvinistic interpretation, one that would harmonize with humanistic views and help eliminate tension between the secular state and the religious feelings of the individual, is essential for Judaism in Israel. Only a humanistic and tolerant religious understanding of Judaism will solidify the interaction between the Gentile Western world and Israel, while continuing the close familiarity, as Talmon describes it, between European national movements and Zionism, the richest of them all.[64]

— 3 —
Quo Vadis Orthodoxy

"Holy" Criminal Violence

Moshe Eliyahu, proprietor of the "Garden of Eden" coffee-house in Petah Tikva, has indeed suffered more than his share at the hands of the haredim: they have destroyed his business and wrecked his furniture. Eliyahu's crime was keeping his shop open on the Sabbath to serve as a meeting place for some of the older members of the Iraqi Jewish community, who like to drop in for a chat and a cup of coffee. On the morning of Saturday, March 10, 1984, the coffee shop was vandalized by prominent members of the religious community, including the Chief Rabbi of Petah Tikva—who had received his appointment by virtue of a law passed in the Knesset.

This violent incident was the punishment for Eliyahu's ignoring the suggestion that he close his business on the Sabbath and obtain reparations from religious groups.[1] An eyewitness said it looked as though a grenade had been tossed into the coffeehouse. Chairs were smashed and windows shattered as the thugs went about their job. They sang rousing Hassidic songs as they methodically destroyed everything in sight.[2]

On April 18, 1984, a resident of the Mea Shearim was arrested as a suspect in an arson attack on a hamam, or Turkish bathhouse, that has been a fixture in Jerusalem's Bukharan Quarter for more than a century. Soon after, dozens of haredim set fire to a clothing store belonging to the owners of the hamam, the Kovshi family, themselves Orthodox, and who keep the hamam rigidly segregated.[3]

About one thousand haredim paraded from the court-house where the suspect was tried for arson against the store in Geula, a residential quarter in Jerusalem. In addition to the vandalism, threatening letters were sent to the Kovshi family, demanding that they shut down their bathhouse "to preserve Jewish values." Press reports quoted comanager Shimon Kovshi as saying that the haredim want to take over the building for a yeshiva. He has been sleeping on the premises every night for the past ten months. "Nobody will insure us anymore. What if the place burns down?"

The geographic limits of haredi actions are expanding.[4]

On April 7, 1984, a Saturday night, Yitzhak Kiali cele-brated a birthday party in an apartment belonging to some of his women friends. Kiali, a graduate student at Jerusalem's Hebrew University, had been wounded in the Lebanon war, and the party also celebrated his recovery. A journalist describes the event: "Unrestrained haredim gathered near the house, screaming madly, rattling the windows, shouting insults and curses. They destroyed trees and smashed a window with a stone."[5] Eyewitnesses said they heard the religious hooligans shouting comments like, "It's a pity you weren't killed in Lebanon!" Then they pressured the neighborhood grocer not to sell goods to the inhabitants of the building who had "dared" to host the party. The apartment happened to be on Keren Kayemet Street near Rehavia, one of Jerusalem's oldest suburbs. There had never been anything brash about Rehavia.

In the fifties, when I was a student, I lived in Jerusalem's Mekor Baruch neighborhood. It was a quaint and quiet area, and the majority of the residents were of deeply rooted Sephardic origin. Today its character is completely different. Six young haredim crashed an enlistment party at a local social club, assaulted many of the guests, and damaged the property. One of the guests was hit on the head by a rock; others were also injured. This time the religious thugs were brought to trial and convicted.[6]

These occurrences are not out of the ordinary. It's seldom that a week, much less a month, goes by without some violence from the Orthodox against the part of the public known as "secular."[7]

Attacks on persons and property occur throughout Jerusalem—in the middle-class, mixed secular and modern Orthodox neighborhood of Rehavia and in the once predominantly Sephardic and traditional quarter of Mekor Baruch, as well as in the ultra-Orthodox bastions of Mea Shearim and Geula. The violence has also extended beyond Jerusalem, not only to the ultra-Orthodox enclave of Be'nei Brak, but to other, less religious locations.

Mindless violence, including the stoning of cars, has become routine in Jerusalem. "Mixed" couples are a favorite target for the special units among the Orthodox, which handle these affairs by "passive explanation"—that is, nonviolent psychological pressure—as well as "punishment."

Rabbi Kahane's Kach party apparently took a break from its activity on the West Bank and recently published an astounding announcement. Jewish women were instructed not to defile themselves and not to bring disgrace on themselves by having contact with Gentiles (non-Jews). Jewish men were called upon to join the "Jewish guardians of honor."[8] It is no wonder that pogroms against "mixed" couples are a widespread phenomenon. But this hooliganism receives wide public support, and the police are helpless.[9]

A group of haredim claim that a tourist hotel in Tiberias is being built on a Jewish gravesite. Bank Leumi is financing the hotel. Although the project received a clean bill of health from the rabbinical authorities, Bank Leumi offices throughout the country have been vandalized and firebombed in an attempt to dissuade the bank from continuing its "desecration." A boycott was recently launched against it, and cheques from the ultra-Orthodox are frequently stamped: "Not to be cashed at Bank Leumi."

At times the mindless attacks cause public conflicts— the Petach Tikva events regarding the opening of the Heichal cinema on the Sabbath and (religious) holidays; demonstrations against autopsies; and physical blocking of areas to prevent people traveling on the Sabbath. These events have claimed the lives of several people, including the well-known sculptor David Polombo, who designed and created the magnificent wrought iron gate in front of the Knesset building, and who was brutally beheaded by the "Sabbath guillotine."

The essence of Orthodoxy's vicious influence, however, is that it creates an atmosphere of terror. This becomes so intense that it erupts inside the religious camp itself. Religious extremism was essentially responsible for the antagonism toward deviant Jews within the religious circle. The obvious religious victims were the moderately Orthodox wearers of the knitted skullcaps, many of whom belong to the NRP, a party that created the climate of religious coercion in Israel. This climate in turn led to the enactment of laws permitting religious coercion. Now they are the victims of a regime that they themselves established.

Religious violence has, however, a wide range of targets. Knesset member Menachem Porush, one of the leading personalities of the haredi non-Zionist Agudat Yisrael faction, was attacked by members of an opposing haredi group.[10] He was seriously injured and had to be hospitalized. Rabbi Porush preferred not to involve the police, so no one was arrested.

In the haredi Mea Shearim neighborhood, a dispute broke out between the Neturei Karta and a haredi group, and the tension heightened. A kiosk was burned down on Malkei Yisrael Street, which is inside the area influenced by the haredim. The owner had been warned to stop selling "secular" newspapers. When the warnings went unheeded, sentence was passed, and the kiosk went up in flames. Needless to say, the kiosk owner now refrains from selling any other than religious papers.

Within a single month, no fewer than three drapery stores inside Jerusalem's haredi areas were burned down. Larry Rogen was religious; nonetheless, his store on the main street of the haredi Mea Shearim quarter was torched three times. It was the thirty-second case of arson in Mea Shearim over an eighteen-month period. Stores and bus shelters were set alight. Not a single case was solved by the police. No one was even brought to trial.

This is terrorism, unadulterated terrorism—and it has triumphed. The Israeli police and security services, the same people who are famed for their fight against Arab terrorism, stand helpless before religious-Orthodox Jewish terrorism.

"Holy" Political Pressure

Having bloodied the rule of law, the rule of Orthodoxy stands unbowed. Its power and influence extend far beyond the visible and spectacular incidents of intimidation and violence. For example, Jerusalem has a relatively liberal law governing the closure of places of entertainment on the Sabbath. Nevertheless, Mayor Teddy Kollek, who is widely known for his tolerance and openmindedness, does not encourage the opening of cinemas on Friday nights. The unfortunate result of this misplaced tolerance has been Jerusalem's transformation into a cultural desert on the Sabbath and religious holidays, to the detriment not only of the city's residents but also of the vital tourist industry. Beginning Thursday evening, as the city prepares for its descent into Sabbath gloom, tourists flee the capital in search of more congenial surroundings. Less mobile than tourists, Jerusalem's residents have to make do with television, forgoing leisure activities outside their homes, which are barred to them on the one day of rest when they are free to pursue them.

After the Six Day War of 1967, Jerusalem was envisaged as becoming a center of culture and creativity. Instead, religious restrictions have turned it into a cultural backwater. The capital, originally a provincial town, has grown into a large city. The building rate is tremendous, but its human foundation is eroding. The increase in construction has been accompanied by a decrease in sophistication, bringing with it as it does a population of village Arabs, mostly Moslems, moving with their families closer to their places of work together.

Radical ultra-Orthodoxy encourages the exodus of secular Israelis, transforming Jerusalem from the capital of the State of Israel into the capital of the ultra-Orthodox Agudat Yisrael.[11]

The elected representatives of the haredi Jews are completely open and unabashed about their intentions. One of them, during a public debate with me, stated bluntly that his ultimate aspiration was a haredi Jerusalem, in the most complete meaning of the word.

As long ago as 1963, a well-known journalist uncovered a secret plan devised by the leaders of the haredi community to expand the borders of the "black" (the ultra-Orthodox dress in black) areas of the city. In a survey done at the same time, the journalist noted the aggressive attitude of the Orthodox toward the secular population, and concluded by saying that so far the religious were far and away the winners in the contest for the capital's image. The clericalization of Jerusalem has increased over the years. Paradoxically, it may well be that "liberal" Jerusalem Mayor Teddy Kollek's charismatic rule in itself is the reason for the speed of the process having slowed down significantly.

Traffic Faces Shabbos Barricades

A glance at a current map depicting the streets closed to Sabbath traffic attests to the success of the ultra-Orthodox plan for Jerusalem's clericalization.

Mayor Kollek's liberal rhetoric, his resounding affirmation of coexistence between Jews and Arabs and between the religious-Orthodox minority and the secular majority, tended to obscure the gradual submission of the religious public to the aggressive elements in their midst.

The mayor's attitude toward the religious population illustrated the pragmatic outlook of his own political party in the city council. He was bent on restoring the city's political standing as Israel's capital and developing Jerusalem as a genuine metropolis.

It was Kollek who made the most of the reunification of the city in order to have the dividing walls destroyed. It was Kollek who inculcated a sense of security in Jerusalem's Arab population. He wove the Arabs into the framework of the municipal mechanism and even succeeded in persuading them to participate in municipal elections. Kollek founded a great fund-raising project, the Jerusalem Foundation, and then used it to overcome the fiscal limitations that had always impeded the city's development. Kollek's vigorous attitude enabled the authorization of grand architectural projects like the Mamilla renovation, the reconstruction of Yemin Moshe and Mishkenot Sha'anim, and the building of luxury hotels and sweeping, colorful parks.

Demographic issues were not the top priority of the energetic mayor, who preferred more tangible projects. He regarded theological and political issues as relatively trivial. Having to deal with a religious-secular problem was an irritant. Kollek felt that fund-raising for the physical renewal and development of Jerusalem had primary importance. Human problems and patterns of lifestyle were at best only secondary, sometimes even marginal, issues. To the contrary, he insisted that the surge of development should not be impeded by the interminable conflicts between religious and secular Jews.

Both as a politician and as a consummately shrewd public servant, Kollek was well aware that the religious-Orthodox population, irrespective of its internal rifts, is a militant, solid entity that has to be brought to heel. Kollek was right to sign the promissory note for the religious public. It would eventually be cashed by his secular electorate. During Kollek's twenty-year reign as mayor of Jerusalem, forty streets have been closed to Sabbath traffic.

Kollek, who began his term of office in 1965, was instrumental in initiating the process of street closing. The process began with a petition brought by the League Against Religious Coercion opposing the closure of King George Street during prayer services at the Great Central Synagogue that dominates its main intersection. The League lost its legal battle.[12]

In retrospect, it is clear that the court appeal defeated its own purpose. Permission to close the road was given ostensibly to facilitate the safe dispersion of the large congregation; it was almost a pedestrian mall, enforced only during the time of the service. Obviously the theological defense of "preserving the sanctity of the Sabbath" held no water in the court's decision. This is irrefutably proved by the fact that to this day the street is reopened to traffic the moment the service ends.

To the religious community, however, this case gave the signal for the gradual closing of the city on the Sabbath. Neighborhoods where roads were closed to vehicular traffic on the Sabbath began to observe, sometimes by dint of force, a pattern of ritual living that was imposed willy-nilly on all its residents. Jerusalem, "united" after the Six Day War, was again divided; not, as formerly, between the west and the east, but this time between the north (where the Orthodox reside) and the secular south, which lives in the creeping shadow of religious encroachment. It is in this odd way that large sectors of the religious-Orthodox public carry out the commandment of isolation from the Gentile and from the Jew "who does not keep the Sabbath."[13]

This situation is not as uncomplicated as it seems. Contrary to accepted opinion, the haredi public is not isolated. The so-called Zionist NRP, which unctuously preaches national integration, established a construction company called "Mash-hab" that actually builds only for the religious Orthodox. It builds ghettos. The residents of these apartments have to sign a legal document to preserve the sanctity of the Sabbath inside the building. The clause is stipulated in any bill of sale. These buildings are "secular free" and state land is readily available to the construction company.[14]

The isolation does not apply only to living quarters. Talmudic halacha as a gauge is not applicable solely to Gentiles: the same law is applicable to Jews "who publicly desecrate the Sabbath" and designates them "mumar l'hakhis"—spiteful apostates. A Jew fitting into the latter category can hardly be called "brother."[15]

The Righteous Jew, the Epikorus, and the Gentile

Talmudic literature describes circumstances in which the apostate, or epikorus, is not worthy of having lost property returned to him.[16]

In principle, any lost item must not be returned to an epikorus, an idolator, or a desecrator of the Sabbath. However, if returning the item also may help in leading toward repentance, then the good deed outweighs the prohibition. This does not make the Sabbath-desecrating Jew kosher. The good Jew should still avoid him—indeed, it is doubtful whether the epikorus should even be invited for a meal. He may be fed only on grounds of pity and charity. If these are the only reasons, then, for according hospitality to the secular person who publicly desecrates the Sabbath, it is hardly worth living in the same neighborhood with him.[17]

Rabbi Shaul Israeli, a judge in the Supreme Rabbinical Appeal Tribunal, also teaches halacha at the well-known Mercaz Ha'Rav yeshiva. He suggests that good Jews who observe the commandments should concentrate themselves in locations where the population is kosher. To avoid any doubt, he suggests avoiding "rotten people." Rabbi Haim David Halevy, Chief Rabbi of Tel Aviv, says that an epikorus who desecrates the Sabbath is suspect and not to be trusted. With all these injunctions, therefore, it is hardly surprising that the religious Jew is commanded to avoid the epikorus throughout his life.[18]

Spending a weekend in Jerusalem would prove the extent of Orthodox influence even in neighborhoods not closed off with chains and Sabbath barriers. The Jerusalem bylaw applying to performance of cultural events does not forbid cinema and theater performances on the Sabbath. But that is only a legal provision. The reality is sharper.

Yitzhak Kariv, a religious man, was mayor of Jerusalem in the fifties. While in office he pushed through a bylaw controlling the opening and closing of businesses, with specific provision for the Sabbath. The bylaw defines a business as a place where business is contracted, including the sale of tickets for cultural events. The city council thus wanted to obstruct the sale of tickets before the Sabbath, although the law has no provisions against the actual performance.

So in the isolated, provincial Jerusalem before the great unification of 1967, cultural and educational events could be held on the Sabbath, and one could go to concerts and movies without any slick and complicated dealing. One simply followed the clear directives of the law. This is not the place for a detailed analysis of the legality that made this possible; we simply want to show that it indeed was possible.

However, the municipality of Jerusalem led by Mayor Kollek proved that legal niceties and practical politics are two different things. When Jerusalem's Journalists House, Beit Agron, opened its doors Saturdays for "morning service" movies, the municipality was asked to adjudicate and came down on the side of Orthodoxy. Beit Agron gave in.

The event is not unprecedented. The municipal archives houses scores of documents recording the Sabbath conflicts of the thirties and even earlier. Interestingly, at that time cinema performances indeed were held on the Sabbath.

In 1987, following similar trends in other parts of the country, some "courageous" cinema owners in Jerusalem opened their premises to the public also on Friday evenings, which under Jewish ritual law are considered the Shabbos eve. A well-organized religious-Orthodox political establishment opposed this change in the status quo by a series of demonstrations. Teddy Kollek, in his official capacity as mayor of Jerusalem, took sides in this encounter: He ordered a criminal suit to be filed in the local court against the few cinema owners in town whose theaters were open on Friday evenings.[19]

The final result, as far as the legal encounter is concerned, was surprising—at least to Kollek and his religious-Orthodox partners. The court did not punish the cinema owners. On the contrary, the court decided that Kollek's request to stop the theaters from opening on Shabbos eve was contradictory to the main legislature. The Municipalities Ordinance, which is considered a kind of "little constitution" regulating the activities of local governments in Israel, gave no power whatsoever to a city council to restrict commercial or cultural activities for ritual or other religious reasons.

The Jerusalem bylaw, as far as ritual-religious restrictions are concerned, was declared "ultra vires" and void "ab initio."

As usual, however, this constitutional decision did not stop the erosion of civil rights regarding freedom from religious sanctions in Israeli life.

While the Supreme Court decided in the famous Shalit case[20] the question of "Who is a Jew," disregarding religious concepts, the Supreme Court's decision was almost immediately overruled by the Knesset, surrendering to the religious-

Orthodox ultimatum.[21]

While the same Supreme Court decided in favor of freedom from ritual dietary law—declaring that local government restrictions on nonkosher meat were outside the power of a city council's bylaw—this Supreme Court decision was also overruled by the Knesset as a result of religious-Orthodox political pressure.[22]

A similar step is under way to overrule the court decision concerning Shabbos cultural events.

The closing of streets instituted by Mayor Kollek began the de-legitimization of the non-Orthodox way of life in the city, and there has been no looking back. It is enough to have a few Orthodox families clustered in a secular area, and to have a few violent incidents such as those described earlier, for the closed-street area to widen its circumference. The Orthodox violence in Rehavia proves this.

Even spheres of life usually regarded as removed from those of the ultra-Orthodox suffer serious, not to mention dangerous, interference through submission to their demands. Hospitals are a shocking, costly example. The Hadassah Medical Association has been forced to hire Gentile-driven vehicles to ferry essential employees to and from work on the Sabbath. An elaborate system of Sabbath elevators was developed.[23] They move automatically, stopping at every floor, throughout the Sabbath, at great cost and concomitant waste of electricity. At the Shaare Zedek Hospital, even public telephones are disconnected on the Sabbath.[24]

At first glance, this appears to be a parochial issue, relating only to Jerusalem. But the first glance is wrong. Jerusalem simply was the first site of victory for the halachic approach; it is just as strong elsewhere now. Although local circumstances play a certain role, the weakness of the local authorities and the strength of the coalition arrangements in the Knesset and in the cabinet give the religious groups freedom throughout Israel.

The best of intentions—as in the case of Shaare Zedek, which certainly applies halachic injunctions as best it understands them—are not enough. Nevertheless, even at Shaare Zedek, the religious public devotes enormous attention to the subject. For example, there is the problem of treating patients on the Sabbath, of traveling in order to transport a sick person on the Sabbath, and for visiting the ill on the Sabbath.

There is also a scholarly halachic debate as to what extent a Jewish doctor and medic are free to treat a patient on the Sabbath when there does not exist an immediate danger to life. As well as why, and under what circumstances, medical treatment may be rendered to a Gentile by a Jewish doctor, or to a Sabbath-desecrating Jew, in general, and on the Sabbath in particular.

The halachic majority opinion is that saving a Gentile life is not considered a "mitzvah"; although it is not considered a humanitarian act either.[25]

But, in practical terms, the halachic ruling is more conciliatory, whereby saving the life of a Gentile on the Sabbath, or that of a Jew desecrating the Sabbath in public, justifies Sabbath violation.[26]

The logic behind these rabbinical rulings cannot be ignored. In order to administer reasonable medical treatment on the Sabbath, a Jew must violate fundamentalistic Sabbath regulations. This conflict has caused the Jews to be grouped in several categories in regard to their "fitness" to be patients.

A faithful Jew has full blessing for medical treatment on the Sabbath while his or her life is in danger.

An "unwillingly" non-observant Jew (Tinok shenishba) is generally exempted from religious sanctions while his or her life is in danger.

An epikorus, a declared secularist, a heretic, a declared member
of a Jewish non-Orthodox religious congregation, or a
Jew affiliated with a Jews for Jesus sect, does not have
to be saved, but again, in practical terms, there exists
a presumption that as long as the contrary is not proved,
every Jew is a righteous one.

Saving a Gentile's life is also subject to pragmatic reasoning.[27] A Gentile who is in immediate danger of losing his
or her life can be saved even on the Sabbath; not based on
the philosophy of "love thy neighbor," but motivated by *netivey
shalom* (preserving peace with neighboring Gentiles), or by
darkey eivah (avoiding atrocities of Gentiles against Jews).

It is not the human dimension that motivates the command to save a life in this respect, but a dimension beneficial
to the ethnocentric community that will remove ammunition
from antagonists of Orthodox Judaism.

Several learned rabbis and lay halachic researchers have
gone into the issue of visiting the sick. Rabbi Haim Bernstein
advises that the Sabbath desecrator be cast out of the Jewish
brotherhood and receive no charity. He does add a fringe
of gentleness: If the desecrator is only suspected of Sabbath
transgression, it is obligatory to visit him.[28]

Another researcher, Rabbi A. Sherman, made a special
survey of the issue of saving the life of a transgressor on
the Sabbath. He poses the question—existential in the light
of Israeli reality—of whether a religious soldier should stand
guard duty on the Sabbath, as he may well be guarding the
lives of Sabbath desecrators. Graciously, Rabbi Sherman
believes that a soldier can obey an order and do guard duty
even if some of his fellows are secular. It is not so much
the decision as the reasoning that is interesting. Rabbi Sherman
bases his approval on the fact that the religious Sabbath

observer is looking ahead to the possibility that the Sabbath desecrators or their children may repent and return to Orthodox belief, "the real Judaism."[29]

Then, too, we have the situation that emergency medical attention, including searches for missing psychiatric patients and urgent operations, are not carried out at Shaare Zedek Hospital unless they fall into the category of halachic "saving of life." In one tragic case, a psychiatric patient was left to wander around unsupervised on a Sabbath. He could neither receive nor make calls to his family since the telephones were all disconnected, and he disappeared.[30]

Clericalization also affects art. When it comes to censorship, Israel doesn't appear to have many problems. The Ministry of the Interior does include a body known as the Council for Film and Play Critique, but its rulings have been quite reasonable, and there has been little friction. There is, of course, the ruling of the High Court of Justice and also that of the Attorney General. They usually take care of any problems, and their decisions on the whole are generous.

But Israel is in the throes of a Kulturkampf that will also establish the future cultural framework of the state. Echoes of the struggle are already audible. This is not the place to go into the pitiful incident when Barbra Streisand ordered that her film *Yentl* should not be shown in Petach Tikva on the Sabbath. The influence of the religious-Orthodox groups was very clear.

Continuous pressure from the ultra-Orthodox, and frequently from the so-called modern Orthodox as well, has severely restricted cultural creation and consumption. This takes two main forms: restrictions on the right to hold performances on "days of rest," and unofficial censorship and economic coercion.

In January 1984, the then-governing Likud bloc, under

pressure from the religious parties, adopted a Knesset resolution condemning cultural activities on the Sabbath, and warned that this was a danger to the preservation of the Jewish heritage. The proposal raised by Knesset member Rabbi Haim Druckman was unprecedented: "The fear as a result of the phenomenon damaging the fundamental values of Judaism, the nation and the State in theatrical as well as various cultural and literary stage presentations [makes us] view them as a danger in the moral deterioration of our society in different spheres."[31]

Yehoshua Sobol, one of the very few Israeli playwrights to have achieved international fame, recently had his latest play, *The Messiah,* open in Haifa. After vociferous charges from Orthodox circles of being anti-religious, the play was on the verge of being banned. Neither the Labor Party majority on the city council nor the labor mayor made a murmur. The situation was finally resolved by the intervention of President Herzog, who suggested that several allegedly blasphemous passages be excised from the script.

A similar incident occurred in Jerusalem, where the head of the local religious council was incensed at the proposed presentation of a play he disapproved of. Rather than merely expressing his opinion, the outraged council member went directly to the owner of the hall where the play was to be performed. His premises, warned the councilor, would be declared unsuitable for festivities like wedding and bar mitzvah parties. It was no idle threat: "unsuitability" meant the withholding of a kashrut certificate, and little business can be done in any Israeli venue lacking that essential authorization. Since parties like these constituted the owner's main source of income, he was forced to cancel the performance.[32] The incident aroused little attention, a lamentable illustration of the Israeli public's abject surrender to Orthodox intimidation.

What's Mine Is Mine; What's Yours Is Also Mine

At one extreme of Israeli religious Orthodoxy is the Neturei Karta. Its best-known representative is spokesman Rabbi Moshe Hirsch, who is also the group's self-styled "foreign minister."

The Neturei Karta's essential principle is its refusal to recognize the State of Israel. Rabbi Hirsch was recently prosecuted in a Jerusalem court for calling the national flag a "rag."[33] Another recent venture was the production of a special Neturei Karta passport. It emphasizes that the bearer is not a Zionist and does not "support the Zionist state [of Israel]." This is presumably intended to safeguard members of the Neturei Karta from being victimized along with other Jews during terrorist hijackings. It is not known if any member has yet had to put the passport to the test. This fringe group has allies among students, teachers, and supporters of the Toldot Aharon yeshiva in Mea Shearim (old quarter) in Jerusalem, and the Hassidic sect comprising adherents of the Szatmar rabbi. Rabbi Hirsch has told the press, "We do not recognize their laws, but their laws recognize us."[34]

Ordinarily, the remainder of the Israeli religious establishment distances itself from these groups. However, as Rabbi Neriah observed, "They chant the same prayers and wear the same 'tallit'—prayer shawl—as we do." There is clearly a hard Orthodox solidarity on many issues.

At the other end of the Orthodox spectrum are the offshoots of the Mizrachi movement, of all shades of religiosity and political belief. These groups have successfully introduced the clout of the rabbinical establishment into the laws of the State.

Such laws place the authority of the State in the hands of the rabbinate and the religious councils, which adjudicate the personal status of every Israeli Jew according to the

Orthodox interpretaton of halacha. The Mizrachi, in its various metamorphoses, was the moving spirit behind all the coalition agreements that enshrined the religious status quo, except in 1981 when the Agudat Yisrael took over, although not without the full agreement and encouragement of the (NRP) Mizrachi.

The Labor movement's political establishment and progeny credit the Mizrachi with legitimizing Zionism in the eyes of Orthodox Jews, for whom it would otherwise have been suspect.

Various considerations influenced the Labor architects of Israeli statehood in their decision to strengthen the religious Zionists. Pragmatism and opportunism certainly played their part, but we can also assume that the seriousness of the situation in 1948 was a strong factor in persuading them to reach a compromise, known as the "Religious Status Quo."[35]

To conclude the agreement, Orthodoxy was granted a monopoly on Jewish religious life, which included the suppression of non-Orthodox religious streams in Judaism. In return, or so it was hopefully anticipated, the religious Zionists would portray the Labor Zionist camp in the most favorable light to Orthodox Jews around the world.

In any event, the religious-Orthodox Zionists did not deliver the support of the ultra-Orthodox. But they made the most of the opportunity to consolidate their control over religious life and much of the educational system in Israel. In addition, the militant wing of religious-Orthodox Zionism declared itself exempt from secular laws and the principles of tolerance and equality, declaring that its parliamentary representation was intended to serve only as a vehicle for establishing a Jewish state according to halacha. A particularly egregious example is Rabbi Simcha Meron, a senior official in the Ministry of Religious Affairs, who was responsible for the management of the rabbinical family courts. In general, Israeli law strictly prohibits public criticism of government policy by senior civil servants.[36] At a press interview, however, Rabbi Meron expressed his opinion that the state should change its fundamental nature, and that its final form must be the establishment of a "Sanhedrin"—a supreme court and legislature in the post-biblical era. He demanded, too, the use of halacha as public and private law and government of the country by halachic sages. Such a regime would prosecute a new kind of "criminal"—one who swims from a beach frequented by both men and women, one who violates the Sabbath, and even one who opts for secular educaton.[37] When asked what the sentence of these "criminals" would be, Rabbi Meron replied: "The courts would be supplied with all the tools, including the power of enforcement, that the present secular courts now have, and they [the criminals] will be treated like any other criminal."

The "Best" Religious-Orthodox Education

The State Education Act of 1953[38] was considered a victory for the State over the forces of disruption and contention. The authors of the law, Prime Minister David Ben-Gurion and Justice Minister Pinhas Rosen among them, hoped it would be remembered as a historic step in strengthening the renaissance of Jewish statehood.[39] Instead, it ripped the delicately woven social fabric of the new state.

Secular education developed without any clear ideological direction; but the Orthodox religious system coalesced around a radical religious point of view, which evoked hatred of secular life.[40]

Orthodox youth absorb a xenophobic ideology[41] emphasizing the isolation of Israel as a "people that dwells alone."[42] However, the ultra-Orthodox independent stream that inculcates non-Zionist and even anti-Zionist attitudes also receives the bulk of its funds from the State Treasury—even though it teaches its students nothing about that State. It doesn't prepare them, either, for the modern world they live in. These schools virtually eliminate subjects like biology and history from their curricula. Avraham Schwartz, a student at the extremist Toldot Aharon yeshiva in Jerusalem, appeared on television—after leaving the yeshiva and the extremist stream— and described the haredi education he received at the yeshiva as teaching hatred of strangers who are different.[43]

Public religious schools, as opposed to the "independent" haredi educational institutions, are under the aegis of the Ministry of Education and Culture.[44] Section 1 of the Public Education Act reads, "Public religious education means: State education, whose institutions shall be religious in their lifestyle, program of study, teachers and supervisors." The Public Education Act was supposed to eliminate multiple streams in Israeli education.[45] Instead it makes a clear distinction between the two leanings. Section 1 further reads: "Sovereign religious education means sovereign education, but its institutions are religious according to their way of life, curricula, teachers and supervisors."[46] Section 18 reads: "The Council for Religious Education has the power to disqualify for religious reasons a nomination or continuation of service of a headmaster, a supervisor, or a teacher. . . ." There should be no misunderstanding. The term "religious" relates to Orthodoxy only. The Jewish religious non-Orthodox streams for some unknown reason did not appeal this provision. They simply accepted the picture as it was presented to them.

All Conservative and Reform religious schools, however, must be established as part of the public-secular school system.

Israeli law permits a teacher to be disqualified from a public-religious school if a non-religious (read non-Orthodox) leaning is suspected. This is a gross violation of teachers' basic civil rights, because the authorities are entitled to investigate whether the teacher is living a halachic life.[47]

It is worth noting that it is not unusual for a public-secular school to employ staff who are Orthodox, or "ba'alei teshuva"—religious penitents. Even though the parents chose a secular, non-Orthodox religious lifestyle, they are not permitted to demand the dismissal of these teachers as likely to influence the children with their extremist views. Such action would be rejected as a violation of religious freedom. On the other hand, teaching staff working at a public-religious school have to sign a formal declaration attesting to their personal Orthodox lifestyle. Refusal to do this means no permission to work at the school.

In Israel's public-secular schools, students are nurtured on pioneering values with an emphasis on humanism. The current economic freeze, with resources understandably strained, has meant considerable limitations for these schools in almost every sphere. Nevertheless, the ministry recently implemented a "TALI" program for increasing the teaching of Orthodox liturgy and ritual in some secular schools.[48] (TALI is an official program for increasing Jewish religious liturgy for public-secular schools—in practical terms, this means religious Orthodox teachings.) This will be in addition to the courses in Judaism compulsory since 1959. These courses could be interpreted as attempts to wean children away from their secular home environment, and even to alienate them from their secular parents. While this is only an educated guess, the Orthodox education authorities have not come up with any valid reason for adding the courses in the present straitened economic circumstances. The issue is even more suspect because of the recent announcement that the ministry is now planning to introduce yet another course, this time for teachers, in the art of religious teaching. These practices are not exactly conducive to tolerant and mutually respectful coexistence.[49]

The radicalization of education also impinges on Israel's ethnic patterns, emphasizing divisions already present. The goal of the mainly Ashkenazi radical Orthodox is not to integrate the Sephardic Jews, most of whom in any case are traditional or Orthodox, but rather to create an elite, which in its turn will take care of increasing the religious orientation and radicalization of the Orthodox population.[50]

This has led to an extraordinary dichotomy. The Sephardic religious movement, Massoret Yisrael (Tradition of Israel), headed by former NRP strongman Aharon Abu-Hatzeira, opposed the increasing clericalization of public-religious education because the movement felt it would widen the social gap, with Sephardic communities being the victims.[51]

Only 25 percent of the Israeli school-going population attends religious schools, both public and independent. But the significance of the religious influence far outweighs these numbers.

First, the rift in Israeli education is total.[52] Second, the values inculcated in the course of religious education are not only spiritual but also social. The religious-Orthodox public is firmly rooted in a social framework strengthened by the united school system and the religious institutions and public commercial activities encompassed by it.[53]

Many Israelis earn their living merely by being affiliated with the religious sector. This provides enormous benefits. There is employment in the educational system: religious councils; municipal Torah-culture departments; the synagogues, which all require a phalanx of helpers; the supervision of kashrut; management of religious institutions; and anti-missionary organizations.

At the level of higher education, the growth of state-supported yeshiva colleges (religious seminaries) has been phenomenal. Their 1960 enrollment constituted 30 percent of the graduates of public-religious schools. By 1970, this had swollen to 70 percent. The graduates of these yeshiva colleges are the elite of Zionist Orthodoxy. They are the leaders of the group they consider the true representatives of the Jewish people today—the Orthodox population. They state baldly that any accommodation with secular society or secular authority is purely tactical.

This was expressed succinctly during a public debate between Rabbi Neriah and myself. The rabbi said that Judaism—that is, Orthodoxy—did not demand tolerance (*sovlanut*) but sufferance or patience (*savlanut*). This was the rabbi's response to the stoning of cars on Jerusalem's Ramot Road. He had been asked to be present and thus prevent the stoning. He refused.

The Orthodox attempts to project this conciliatory image are completely superficial. Far from being patient, the religious Orthodox are unforgiving, hard, and militant. This is apparent in their determination over the Sabbath struggle, religious ritual, and other divisive factors.

Rabbi Zvi Yehuda Kook did something completely out of Orthodox character when he joined the League Against Religious Coercion upon its establishment in the late forties. This made his gesture all the greater: He wanted to give a concrete example of extreme sufferance. His son (who bears the same name), however, did not follow his father's teaching. He equated the secular attitude with blasphemy, although he simultaneously invested that so-called blasphemy with mystic and holy authority by describing the State of Israel as the coming of golden salvation.

The stimulus that was to transform religious Zionism into militant religious Zionist Orthodoxy was the Six Day War of 1967. It instilled in the movement a sense of sacred mission to redeem the entire biblical Eretz Israel. Ironically for the Orthodox camp, the Six Day War marked the final surrender of pioneering and socialist ideals to the pursuit of materialism.

The trend was intensified by the traumatic experience of the Yom Kippur War. It also brought the religious-Orthodox Zionists closer to the Gahal (later the Likud) coalition of the Herut and right-wing Liberal parties, which also followed the holy grail of the "Greater Land of Israel."[54]

This messianic nationalism within the NRP began as a mild, intraparty revolt by the youth wing. In 1968, the "Young Turks," as the popular press described them, led by Zevulun Hammer and imbued with the ideals of Rabbi Zvi Yehuda Kook, son of the former Chief Rabbi, as well as those of Rabbi Neriah, won 20 percent of the votes in the party's internal elections. In the 1973 Knesset elections following the Yom Kippur War, the Labor Alignment won only 51 seats. The NRP won 10, and although this was a loss of 2 from its pre-election position, it left the party more powerful than before. The Labor Alignment could never have formed a governing coalition without those 10 votes. The NRP had achieved the best result possible—it became indispensable.

As for the Labor Alignment, it was caught in a trap of its own making. It was used to short-term political machination, not the far-sighted and Machiavellian manipulation of the religious Orthodox. In its greed to retain the reins of government, Labor gave the NRP even more sweeping authority than it already held, and forfeited the last chance of braking the momentum of the NRP and the messianic fervor of its various components.

The avalanche began to slide.[55]

Rabbis, yeshiva college principals and teachers, and other religious leaders affiliated with the NRP began the chant: "We shall not surrender a blade of grass in Judea, Samaria, and Gaza."

Gush Emunim was established as an official NRP faction in 1974. It swiftly gathered its own momentum, and by 1981 had broken away from its parent party. The NRP lost control of its golem.

There was a terrible fascination in watching the pattern develop. The religious-Orthodox educational system, which had led to mindless suburban violence, merited the dubious compliment of producing steadily more sophisticated thinking that culminated in Jewish terrorism.

Rabbi Meir Kahane and his Kach movement are on the margins of the Orthodox-Nationalist political map.[56] Their Orthodox-religious form of racism is well known. What needs emphasizing is that it is not so much the man or his political success that should be feared. The real danger lies in the increasing and countrywide support for an openly totalitarian approach.

Aside from their burning desire to make Israel Arab-free, Kahane and his followers have given special attention to the Temple Mount in Jerusalem.[57]

Ever since the Six Day War, the Temple Mount has been the focus of radicals and mystics, singly and in groups. One of the first incidents was sparked by none other than Rabbi Goren, then Chief Rabbi of the IDF, and later Ashkenazi Chief Rabbi of Israel. In 1967 he announced his intention of praying on the Mount, the former site of the First and Second Temples, and the present site of two of the holiest shrines of Islam—the Dome of the Rock and the al-Aksa mosque. It took an extraordinary meeting of the cabinet in special session to stop the rabbi's valiant urge.

A former member of the Jerusalem City Council, Gershon Solomon, heads a group called the "Guardians of the Temple Mount." They meet annually on Tisha B'Av in a quiet, nonviolent demonstration to obtain permission to pray on the Mount.[58]

In 1969, a deranged Australian tourist, Denis Rowan, set fire to the al-Aksa mosque, causing serious damage. In September 1982, the Ministry of Religious Affairs announced it was beginning excavations at the Mount, without the approval of the responsible authorities, the Antiquities Department of the Ministry of Education and Culture.

In April 1983, an American Jew, Alan Goodman, killed two Moslems and wounded several others when he opened fire on a crowd of Friday worshippers at al-Aksa. He was convicted and sentenced to a prison term.

Ever since the establishment of the state, Jewish underground groups have periodically been exposed. Most of them were religious Orthodox, although one of the earliest cells discovered comprised young haredim, many of them linked to an Agudat Yisrael institution. Others included the present Chief Rabbi, Mordechai Eliyahu, and a leader of the ultra-Orthodox Sephardic community. They represented, of course, the ultra-Orthodox of non-Zionist or anti-Zionist leaning.

Another Jewish underground cell was led by Joel Lerner, an American-born high-school teacher and a lecturer at a yeshiva college in Jerusalem. Lerner's cell was exposed in the seventies. They had planned to damage holy Moslem sites on the Temple Mount. Lerner was a founder-member of the Jewish Defense League, the precursor of Kahane's Kach party.[59]

Lerner's penchant for violent lawbreaking culminated in

his being convicted of planning to plant explosives on the Temple Mount. He was also suspected of having vandalized Christian institutions in Jerusalem. Today, Lerner heads the Institute for Torah in Israel, having apparently left his activist past behind him in order to instill his values into other people.[60]

On August 11, 1982, the gravesites of former Israeli president Yitzhak Ben-Zvi and his wife were found desecrated. Earlier, the gravesite of Theodor Herzl had been found similarly desecrated. Both rather disgusting incidents were traced to an underground haredi group called Keshet. The vandalism was said to be retribution against "Zionist sites" for the archaeological excavations at the City of David dig.

In early 1984, the police disclosed yet another attempt to destroy the Moslem shrines on the Temple Mount. The culprits were an offbeat gang of mystics who called themselves Bnei Yehuda and lived in Lifta, a village outside Jerusalem. They were not found to have any connection with Lerner, but the incident sounded the alarm. The leader of this gang, Shimon Banda, successfully hid for some time, until he was finally arrested, convicted, and sentenced to eight years of imprisonment by the Jerusalem District Court.

The Temple Mount drew the attention of the entire Moslem world, and in many ways was regarded as a test of Israel's claims to offer freedom of religion and its assurance of protection to followers and institutes of all faiths. Israeli police and security services were finding it progressively more difficult to make good on that affirmation.

As it happened, in April 1983 the LaRouche *Executive Intelligence Review* reported that the attacks were inspired by elements hostile to the international interests of the United States.[61] These elements were deliberately inciting a religious-racist conflagration centering on control of the Temple Mount. The report was published precisely one year before the disclosure of the biggest Jewish underground terror group yet, after another attempt to demolish the Moslem shrines on the Mount. Almost all the suspects were Jewish settlers living in Judea and Samaria.

The *Executive Intelligence Review* reporter maintained that the plot to destroy the shrines had already been under way for more than a year. He maintained that the principals controlling the entire operation were specific Christian institutions assisted by fanatical Zionist factions in Israel and the West Bank. He claimed they were deliberately trying to stir up political confusion that would incite a worldwide holy war against American allies and interests abroad. The reporter bolstered his claim with a description of the groups he believed to be behind the plan, among them certain Torah study institutes.

Quite aside from this claim, one cannot ignore the support given by the Israeli government to those Torah institutes with mystic and extremist nationalist leanings.

Meanwhile, a series of violent events shook the West Bank. A rumor swept the area that Jewish settlers had poisoned all the wells. The Arab population was almost hysterical, and the tension that began to increase in the spring (Passover) of 1983 remained high for almost a year.

In one incident a young girl was fatally shot by a settler associated with Gush Emunim. Meir Harnoi was convicted of manslaughter by the Tel Aviv District Court and given a ten-year jail sentence.

In January 1984, a cache of grenades was discovered in a Moslem cemetery near the Temple Mount, and a Jerusalem church was damaged in an attack similar to the torching of a Baptist church in the summer of 1983. That attack itself was reminiscent of an attack on a much wider scale twenty years earlier, when one thousand yeshiva students went on a wild rampage against Catholic churches in Jaffa, Haifa, and Jerusalem.

The grenade cache was traced back to May 1980, when a meeting of settlers decided to attack the Arab mayors of seven West Bank towns. It was described as retribution for the murder one month previously of six Jewish settlers outside Beit Hadassah in Hebron. Three of the targeted mayors were deported before the plan was activated. The first attack failed. The second was successful. Nablus Mayor Bassam Shaka lost both legs and Ramallah Mayor Karim Khalaf one leg in two separate car bomb explosions. The mayor of El-Bireh escaped injury, but an IDF Druse sapper was blinded while trying to defuse a bomb planted outside the mayor's garage. Settler members of the underground were responsible for all the attacks.

In the 1983 rampage, about one hundred yeshiva students were arrested, but the public remained passive because they were, after all, members of only a "marginal group."

Are recent events the price we pay for that tranquil attitude? Has anyone considered instilling values of tolerance and humanism into those religious educational institutions as a quid pro quo for continuous financial support from the despised Zionist government? Or is there some misapprehension about the spirit already in the hearts of these "nice" youngsters who storm out on impulsive pogroms? Do we approve of this religious nationalist generation that has succeeded the socialist pioneers?

There was no justification for complacency in the continuing wave of Jewish terrorism. On October 29, 1982, grenades were left on the soccer field of a Hebron school. One exploded and two schoolboys were injured.

After the murder in Hebron of yeshiva student Aharon Gross in July 1983, the terrorists struck at the Islamic College in Hebron. In gangster style, two men with their faces hidden by red-checkered keffiyehs sprayed the entrance and courtyard of the college with gunfire and grenades, and then escaped in a car. Three students were killed and several injured.

On December 20, 1983, a gang of three Jewish terrorists left a plastic bag containing grenades near the Sheikh al-Rashid mosque in Hebron. The guard was seriously injured, but the gang had aimed for more than one casualty: The explosion had been intended to coincide with the end of a prayer service. Fortunately, the service had ended earlier than usual, and the congregation had dispersed before the explosion took place.

The saga of this terrorist group ended with the booby-trapping of five Arab buses in the East Jerusalem terminal. Israeli security services discovered the bombs in time to defuse them, preventing what would have been carnage. The following day, police announced the discovery of a large terrorist network among the West Bank settlers.[62]

The suspects have claimed they were forced to act on their own because of the so-called impotence of the Israeli security services in the face of Arab attacks on Jewish settlers and travelers on the West Bank. It is not known what deeper motivations these Jewish terrorists may have had.

There appears to have been virtually a conspiracy of silence, a reluctance to probe too far. The obvious common denominator among all the suspects was militant, nationalist, religious Orthodoxy, and this highly significant fact was ignored.[63] Too many Israeli politicians make light of the inherent danger in religious Orthodoxy and the threat it poses for the future of democratic rule in Israel.

The politicians examine Orthodoxy through the lens of shtetl and casbah folklore, repressing or overlooking the political currents and inclinations that flow from Talmudic understanding. They regard Joel Lerner, the Lifta gang, and the bus bombers simply as deviants suffering from a kind of Orthodox adolescent acne. They are "lovers of Zion" and hence worthy of forgiveness.

The Jewish underground, whose members were convicted in 1985, put a new phenomenon before public view. The attitudes of the terrorists clearly were rooted in the consciousness of many people in the various religious-Orthodox camps.

Allow me to introduce:

Accused #1: Menachem Livne, commander of the organization and said to have founded it. His family background is haredi Judaism. His father was a functionary with the Agudat Yisrael. Livne studied at an independent haredi school affiliated with the Agudat Yisrael and continued at the Noam Seminary at Pardess Chana. He later went to the Mercaz Ha'Rav yeshiva, which seems to have graduated so many militants.

Accused #2: Yehuda Etzion, who led the establishment of the settlement of Ofra in Samaria in 1975 and later became prominent as a leader of Gush Emunim. He was charged with planning the attacks, especially those on the West Bank mayors and on the mosques. Etzion was a founder of the prototype West Bank settlement of Elon Moreh, and is now a member of religious Kibbutz Be'eria near Safad.

Accused #3: Shaul Nir, a student of the public-religious school system. He lives in Kiryat Arba, was an aide-de-camp to Rabbi Moshe Levinger, active in buying houses in Hebron. He was directly involved in the mosque plot, the soccer field grenades, and the attack on the Islamic College.

Accused #4: Yehoshua Ben-Shoshan, widely known for his religiosity and his profession. He is a ritual circumciser and lives in Kiryat Arba. His house in Jerusalem was claimed to have been a base used by the terrorists. He was accused of murder, attempted murder, and membership in a terrorist organization.

Accused #5: Yitzhak Gaveiram, one of the religious settlers who moved up to the Golan Heights. He played a less significant role in the underground, although he was initially also accused of murder and indirect assistance to the terrorist organization.

Accused #6: Benzion Heinman, a friend of Rabbi Levinger (both were members of Moshav Nahalim near Petach Tikva). He is known for his active participation in most of the Gush Emunim illegal settlement activity during Labor's term of office. He was charged with participation in the plan to destroy the Temple Mount mosques, the attack on the mayors, and membership in the Jewish terrorist underground.

Accused #7: Ya'acov Heinman, younger brother of Benzion and a pilot in the Israel Air Force; also accused of membership in the terrorist organization.

Accused #8: Dan Be'eri, a French Catholic who converted to Judaism. He is the only member of the Jewish underground who also was associated with Joel Lerner's Hasmonean movement and acted as a connecting link between the two organizations. He was almost totally preoccupied with the construction of the Third Temple. He had dedicated himself to studying the ritual to be performed there, and to this end was associated with the Ateret Cohanim yeshiva that specializes in this issue. Be'eri had moved to the Old City of Jerusalem to be able to see Mount Moriah every day. His intense religious belief convinced him that he was destined to serve in the Temple. He was charged with membership in a terrorist organization and with carrying out technical projects for it.

Accused #9: Ze'ev Friedman, a resident of Kiryat Arba. He was charged with participation in the plot to blow up the Temple Mount mosques.

Accused #10: Haim Ben-David, an amateur archaeologist from the Golan Heights who was also charged with participation in the Temple Mount plot.

Accused #11: Uzi Sharpaf, accused of membership in a terrorist organization. He is a son-in-law of Rabbi Moshe Levinger and the only non-Ashkenazic member of the terrorist organization. He was particularly noted for his intense religiosity and total dedication to his holy studies. He was charged with murder.

There were twenty-five accused in all, among them the son of Ya'acov Heinman; Shaul Nir's brother; and Menachem Neuberg, son-in-law of Rabbi Waldman, one of the leaders in the Tehiya party and head of the Nir yeshiva college in Hebron where Neuberg was a student.

During the police investigation the two most prominent leaders of the Jewish settlement movement in Hebron, Rabbis Levinger and Waldman, were summoned to police headquarters in Jerusalem. Both have close connections with several of the accused, including, of course, their respective sons-in-law, Sharpaf and Neuberg.

Rabbis Levinger and Waldman were not tried, and hence the material on their investigations was not made public. Only after a generation has passed will the archives disclose to historians details of events that are so disturbing to the public today. The accused were sentenced to varying prison terms. Some of them turned state's evidence, so many of the questions about the Jewish underground will remain unanswered. Even before completion of the investigation and before sentences had been passed on all the accused, the dam broke, and the right-wing groups, including the religious-Orthodox establishment, began calling for a pardon.

Yitzhak Shamir, now head of the Likud bloc and then minister of foreign affairs, told the demonstrators that he identified with their request for a pardon. The laws of division of authority between state and religion were damaged and the law of sub judice was breached. A group of Knesset members—including Haim Kaufman, at the time head of the Likud bloc in the Knesset; Rabbi Druckman of the Morasha party and now again a member of the NRP; and Geula Cohen of the Tehiya party—led a move to table a special bill granting a blanket pardon to all the accused.

Results of a public opinion poll showed support for a pardon from almost all Kahane supporters, from 86 percent of Likud supporters, and, apparently, from half of the Alignment supporters interviewed. All eyes were on the president, the only person legally entitled to grant pardons. There were violent demonstrations, which served only to increase the fame of the underground. President Herzog declared publicly that he would not be pressured.

Only the minority remained calm, and a few people organized a move in defense of the judicial institutions of the State against public pressure. Many an eyebrow was raised when the religious kibbutz movement came out in support of the president and, consequently, state sovereignty. The movement issued a formal announcement urging Herzog not to grant the pardon. This could not have been easy in the face of the announcement by Sephardic Chief Rabbi Mordechai Eliyahu supporting the convicted underground members and demanding their freedom "in order to return them to their homes so they can educate their children." For the first time there was clear evidence that much of the Israeli public from all strata and headed by religious Orthodox leadership was unhappy with the principle of equality before the law. The attitude of this large section of the public could be said to hold that people who attack Arabs and plan to destroy Islamic shrines are not like other criminals in Israel.

Professor Yuval Ne'eman of Tehiya, a former minister of science and technology, and Rabbi Neriah publicly expressed a certain understanding of the motives of the underground.

A short time later, a symposium was held in Jerusalem. The subject was, "How Did We Get to the Jewish Underground?" Professor Ephraim Urbach was a main speaker. He said, "One must strongly oppose Gush Emunim for its chauvinist, nationalist belief that drapes itself in religious garb. People from Gush Emunim speak as if they know the will of Providence and are destined to carry it out. They believe that they stand above the law, and that a law not supporting their views is invalid."[64]

Some had perceived the problem much earlier. In the sixties, Yitzhak Gruenbaum, Israel's first minister of the interior, called Israel a democracy ruled by theocratic laws.[65] He was right. The two original concessions that gave the situation statutory validity occurred in 1953. The first was the Act on the Jurisdiction of the Rabbinical Courts, which gave the Orthodox Rabbinate total control over marriage and divorce. The second was the State Education Act, which entrenched Orthodox control over a large percentage of Israel's youth.

The results of this abdication of authority have become apparent. In this context, it is worth quoting President Herzog, who remarked that if there is a Jewish underground, we must reexamine our educational system.

According to Shoshana Beyer, a senior official at the Ministry of Education and Culture, the ministry has no intention whatsoever of establishing a study program on tolerance. Could this be an addendum to the comment of Rabbi Zvi Moshe Neriya that for him religious-Orthodox Judaism means not tolerance but patience? And who, if not the students of Rabbi Neriya, are today heads of the Ministry of Education and Culture?

Israeli nationalism has made a contract with religious Orthodoxy, and it can be said that former prime minister Menachem Begin's actions, and those of his successors, abandoned the teachings of the secular Jabotinsky in favor of the clericalization of the people. This protected them against attack from opponents on the center and left of the political spectrum, whose leanings toward the rule of law, pluralism, the sovereignty of the nation, and the principles of the Declaration of Independence could be countered in several ways:

1. The belief that, unlike other nations, the Israeli nation has preserved itself through all the generations of Hellenization.

2. The belief that the people of Israel are the Chosen People.

3. The justification of violence against the Arabs living among us.

4. Settlement while pushing out the Arab inhabitants.

5. Sovereignty over the Temple Mount.

6. The study of Jewish religious-Orthodox consciousness as an expression of the wholeness and continuity of the nation.

These are no longer the opinions of fringe groups. The already wide gap between two cultures and two ways of life without any common denominator is increasing steadily.

Let there be no misunderstanding. It is not Gush Emunim or Rabbi Kahane or the religious parties and their institutions that are being weighed in the balance. The very existence of the Zionist state—the policies of Herzl and Borochov, of Ruppin and Jabotinsky—is at stake for the verdict of history.

Several days after Kahane was first elected to the Knesset, I met an acquaintance in the streets of Jerusalem. We discussed various issues, and more or less in summary of them all, he said: "You know, Kahane expressed what many of us thought in our hearts but did not dare say out loud."

In his memoirs, Raymond Aron discussed the contrast between religious belief, which fulfills the human need for an explanation of reality, and the dogma of the secular religions of Marxism, Leninism, and National Socialism. I am not convinced by Aron's distinction. At least insofar as Judaism is concerned, the 613 Commandments specify everything a Jew must or must not do.

Halacha is the "Torah of Life," and according to the practice of the various Orthodox sects and traditions it is fixed and immutable. Such worldviews necessarily exhibit a lack of tolerance to all others, especially toward those with a so-called secular and agnostic outlook.

It is mystical worldviews like these that seek to rule our minds and our national life today.

— 4 —
The Place Where
They Must Take You In

Home is the place where, when you have to go there,
They have to take you in.
 —Robert Frost, "The Death of the Hired Man"

Repatriation, Citizenship, and Nationality

In the midst of a tragic controversy are the Diaspora Jews, dragged there by the State of Israel itself.

The twentieth day of the month of Tammuz (July 5) commemorates the death of Theodor Herzl, visionary and founder of the Jewish state. The Knesset selected this day to enact the Law of Return, promising the right of repatriation—return to the homeland—to every Jew.[1]

On July 5, 1950, David Ben-Gurion spoke during the debate preceding the enactment of the new legislation, which he said was intended to bring each and every Jew back to Israel whatever the reason for his desire to be there: "Whether due to deprivation of his rights in the Diaspora; whether due to an uncertain existence because of oppression and expulsion; whether due to hatred and contempt surrounding him; whether due to his inability to live a free and open Jewish life; whether due to his love for an ancient tradition, for the Hebrew culture, and for the sovereignty of Israel."

The legislation coincided with the first wave of immigrants to land on the shores of the newly independent state. They came from the *shuks* and crowded ghettos of Iraq and Yemen, from the tired Balkans, and from the searing deathcamps of Poland.

It was painful, this process that came to be known as *absorption,* and which meant settling these great and disparate masses of people into some kind of orderly existence. Tent camps were established, but the conditions were appalling. Each immigrant was granted citizenship through the Law of Return, and was listed on the population registry as a Jew according to personal declaration of both nationality and religion. The Population Registration Ordinance was a legacy of the Mandate and it was obligatory to note the two designations separately.

Ostensibly all was well—the hard problems of survival outweighed pedantic issues.

Nevertheless, the official directives of the Ministry of the Interior and the personal view and political affiliation of individual ministers began to demonstrate the clash between the Zionist secular culture prevailing from prestate days and the rabbinical Orthodox heritage.

Interior Minister Moshe Haim Shapiro (NRP) stated explicitly in early 1965 that as long as the legal authority to elucidate the word *Jew* rested with his office, as laid down by the Supreme Court, he would determine the definition pronounced by the nation according to his ministerial discretion.[2]

While the Orthodox groups openly acknowledged their adherence to the concept of Jewish religious law as a test of nationality, as state officials they stressed the purported identification between their religious outlook and the popularly accepted secular point of view. They could hardly be accused of clericalizing the Israeli system of handling immigration when reasoning and pretext were secular.

Ilana, Jewish Orphan Born to a Gentile Mother

Ilana Stern was born in a Russian labor camp in the Soviet Union where her father, Wolf Stern, had been incarcerated during World War II as a Polish citizen as well as a Zionist Jew. It was in the camp that he met Ilana's mother, a young Estonian Gentile woman imprisoned for her anticommunist views. Ilana's mother died in childbirth, and the infant was given to a foster family.

Released at the end of the war, Wolf Stern could have returned to Poland, but he was determined to find his daughter. Luck was with him, and the reunited father and daughter went to Poland. Their welcome was anything but warm. Neighbors abused Ilana for her Jewishness—abuse that continued through kindergarten and first grade, where the little girl had her first taste of anti-Semitism. Father and daughter emigrated to Israel in 1956.

Only when 16-year-old Ilana reported for preliminary registration for the IDF did she discover that in the Population

Registry both her nationality and religion were defined as Christian.

Ilana and her father were stunned. This girl, who as the daughter of a Jew had felt the scourge of anti-Semitism, who knew no culture other than that of Judaism and Israel, and who had never undergone the requisite Christian ritual of baptism, was declared a Christian in the state to which she had fled for refuge because she was Jewish.

The Ministry of the Interior had a simple explanation. Jewish religious law holds that anyone who is not born of a Jewish mother, and has not converted to Judaism, is not a Jew. But then Ilana raised the thorny question of just where her supposed Christianity came from. From Jewish law, was the prompt response—her Christianity had been inherited from her mother. She was advised to convert, but she was adamant. Since she held no religious belief of any kind, submitting to the ritual act of conversion would violate her personal convictions.

In Poland, Ilana had not taken the easy way out and converted to Christianity. She had borne her Jewishness proudly. So she did not intend to convert in Israel merely at the whim of some clerk in a government office.

Judicial proceedings began.[3]

One judge publicly and vocally disqualified himself as prejudiced in favor of the claim and reasoning of the Ministry of the Interior. Another judge took over, and experts came to testify, including the religious minister's aide for Christian affairs.

The ministry's stand presumably was based on the minister's 1956 instruction: "Regarding determination of religion, the rule is that a child's religion is determined according to the religion of the mother." The court concluded that although Ilana's mother was not Jewish, her actual religious affiliation was unknown. There was a wide range of possibilities. The Orthodox Provoslavic faith was Estonia's main religion but Catholicism and Protestantism both existed as well. The mother presumably was born in a Gentile home, but Ilana had never been baptized to make her an acknowledged follower of any Christian creed. The court also had to rule on the principal issue of Ilana's having been categorized as a Christian. The court decision was that affiliation with any Christian denomination is not inherited from either parent, but can only be conferred by baptism.

The end result was the decision that, just as Islam is not permitted to define Judaism in its religious meaning, so Jewish theology cannot determine Christianity. Ilana was freed of the "religion-nationality" definition with which she had been labeled by the Population Registry and both affiliations were erased. Ilana unquestionably is not Jewish from the religious point of view, but then again, she doesn't want to be religious anyway.

And what about her national, ethnic Jewishness?

The directives determined by the Israeli government stated: "If one of the parents is a non-Jew, and both parents openly declare that their child is a Jew and not of any other religion, the child is registered as a Jew."[4] Ilana fulfilled the conditions of the declaration.

Nonetheless, the Ministry of the Interior stubbornly refused to give way. Ilana petitioned the Supreme Court for an order *nisi,* and the ministry submitted to the ruling. Ilana was registered as being of Jewish nationality but as having no religion, despite the fact that her mother was known to be a Gentile. Ilana eventually left Israel.

Although Ilana Stern's case was raised only in 1964, the synchronized attack of the Orthodox groups on the secular-national definition of the new immigrants had already begun in 1958 with the large wave of immigrants pouring in from Poland and other Eastern European countries.

The issue was handled methodically and shrewdly by the NRP, and the political nonreligious establishment unwillingly but pragmatically was prepared to accept the NRP's demands. They were already faced with the pressure of coalition agreements.

Toward the end of the fifties a titanic struggle began between two giants—the Talmudic rabbis and the so-called secular Zionists. They committed themselves to a historic battle that would decide the real ideological factor defining the self-determination of the Jewish people—the flexible definition by implication, or the rigid and narrow rabbinical Orthodox definition.

The battle would go to the roots of Jewish existence in Israel, and would have an immediate influence on the Diaspora. At one level it was a struggle between two establishments for the sovereignty of Israel; but in practical terms it was a battle to define the sole representative of the Jewish people— the elected government, or the religious Orthodox establishment.

It would later be noted that at the time very few people understood the implications of the struggle, not only for the future of Israel's constitutional identity but also for the identity and integrity of Jewish people throughout the world.

Ruffeisen, Jewish Survivor of the Holocaust— Is He Jewish?

As in every war, the reason for opening fire was only a secondary issue.

The Ministry of the Interior was then in the hands of Israel Bar-Yehuda, a member of the Ahdut Avodah, the Israel Socialist Party of those times. On March 10, 1958, the minister gave instructions for a nationwide population registration. This would include details received in good faith from each person registered. Although this was not emphasized, the instructions obviously included recording details of religion and nationality.

The minister was guided by the judicial position, which is itself based on the population registry, used as a source of statistical information. But civil rights cannot be determined from the details the registry contains.

The religious establishment went into battle array. Bar-Yehuda's directives were indeed a worthy *casus belli*. By the end of March the subject of these directives was already on the government's agenda.

The logic that guided Moshe Haim Shapiro as minister of religious affairs was completely different from that which he would exhibit seven years later when he would replace Bar-Yehuda as minister of the interior. Seven years later, Interior Minister Shapiro was to tell the public that he would not intervene to alter the regulations. It is interesting to note that the minister of the interior appealed to the same authority awarded to him, while it was under the jurisdiction of a previous minister who held a different point of view.

Ironically, Justice Bernson's decision in the case of Brother Daniel, which was based wholly on secular grounds, supported the religious minister in his clerical stand. Justice Bernson wrote: "The authority . . . regarding the Law of Return, is the Minister of the Interior. . . . He determines who is a Jew."[5]

During those spring days of 1958, the legal argument which was to serve the future religious party ministers was still unknown.

The issue of "directives"—a clear enunciation of how to define the condition of being a Jew—preoccupied the legislature and the judiciary to a point beyond common sense. Here was this fledgling state, desperate to survive, a resented newcomer to the family of nations, and nonetheless devoting itself to the metaphysical problem of just what constituted membership in it.

In Israel, the issue could now very broadly be recognized as a direct conflict between the view of the religious-Orthodox Jews and that of the new secular Israelis.

To the non-Orthodox religious Jewish community in the United States the issue of identifying Jewishness rested solely with lineage.

The NRP countered with Herzl's observation that "we know we belong to the same community only because of our fathers' beliefs." The NRP quickly sensed that the Diaspora Jews were uneasy with the "subjective understanding" of the secular camp. In the struggle with secularism, which holds that it is enough to *feel* Jewish to be a Jew, the NRP could present itself as "the representative of world Jewry."

One would like to give the religious-Orthodox leaders the benefit of the doubt—to say they were holding on to the concept of Jewishness that had held the Jews together since the fall of the Second Temple. To them, the concept of Jewish nationality belonged to an alien Western philosophy. The distinction between religion and nationality is unacceptable to an Orthodox Jew.[6]

The Talmudic-halachic concept of Judaism is ethnocentric by definition. Belief is combined with ethnic roots. Talmudic-halachic Judaism can be easily described as a "people under divine constitution."[7] This constitution (the Bible as legally interpreted during the ages by rabbinical lawyer-sages) is to be obeyed by any Jew apart from his personal emotional involvement or "religiosity."

Orthodoxy means a total legal system that rules Jewish life just as, say, British law governs the life of the queen's subjects. Unlike national law, however, Orthodoxy has no territorial restrictions, so each Jew bears his Talmudic legal code wherever he goes. A Jew is under Talmudic-halachic jurisdiction any time and at any place as long as he is defined by this law as a Jew. His personal belief, affiliation to a non-Orthodox Jewish religious community, or even secularist philosophy are irrelevant to the power Jewish Orthodox law has over his life. Jewish nationality, as far as the Orthodoxy is concerned, is ethnocentric, a view that contradicts the secular, modern polycentric nationalism of the Zionist national movement.[8]

Rather than becoming involved in this dispute over the two concepts of Judaism, the NRP was better off presenting the struggle as between the "shallow materialistic" secularists in Israel and the monopolistic religious Orthodoxy as a moral common denominator for Jewish people all over the world. The proof, the NRP claimed, lay in secular reasoning. This claim of the "right of the new immigrant to declare his Jewishness as he wishes without any criteria to guide him" was merely a superficial formalism.

It was a battle between the guardians of the "true" Judaism, which had been preserved over thousands of years, and the assimilators and rebels against the yoke of the Commandments, this last unquestionably leading to intermarriage and impurity.[9]

The contest left the non-Orthodox Jewish community of the United States openmouthed. They were faced with a choice which they had no intention of taking. The secular attitude was unacceptable to the majority of them, and so long as the conflict was one between secularism and their own prized moral Judaism, they felt it better to remain on the sidelines.

The silence of the Diaspora Jews enabled the government of Israel to compromise and overcome the crucial issue. But although the crisis had passed, the overall result was the fracture of Judaism as a national, pluralistic front, and the term "Shivat Zion"—the Return to Zion—for the first time was limited in outline and understanding.

The religious issue remained controversial.[10]

In 1960, new instructions were issued by the minister of the interior. They indicated further withdrawal from the pluralistic view and total dependence on the religious-law view, while ignoring the demands of interreligious and intercommunal jurisprudence, which were classified in the case of unbaptized and non-Gentile Ilana Stern.

This was the directive for minors:

A. A child born to a Jewish mother and Gentile father will be registered as a Jew in the section [of the questionnaire] on religion and nationality.

B. A child born to a Gentile mother and Jewish father will be registered under "religion" and "nationality" according to the details suitable to the mother. Should the parents oppose registration of the child according to the said details, the child will be registered according to the non-Jewish religion and nationality given by the parents.

C. Should the parents oppose the directives outlined above, and not provide other details of non-Jewish religion and nationality: (1) "Religion" will be entered as "Jewish father, Gentile mother." (2) "Nationality" will not be entered on the questionnaire, nor on the identity card.

D. Should proof be supplied that the child was converted by a certified rabbinical tribunal, the child will be registered as Jewish in the sections for religion and nationality.[11]

The directive of 1960 was in fact regressive and confirmed the clerical aims of the Ministry of the Interior. This directive was put to the test by the petitions of Jewish converts and the Holocaust survivor Oswald Ruffeisen, known as Brother Daniel.[12]

Brother Daniel is a Carmelite monk, born in Kraków, Poland, to Jewish parents. He was educated as a Jew and was active in the Zionist youth movement in Kraków. During the Nazi occupation he worked, as a Jew, together with the Partisans. He was even decorated for his heroism in saving a number of his fellow Jews from death—the risk being all the greater as he himself was a Jew. He took refuge in a Catholic monastery where he was influenced by Christian theology. He converted to Christianity immediately after the war in 1945. After the events of the Holocaust, he decided on a life of seclusion and joined the Carmelite order. He did this, he said, because the order originated from and had its principal location on Haifa's Mount Carmel in Israel, hoping that this would enable him to be transferred to Haifa after joining the order. He actually succeeded in doing so only in 1958.

In a request to the Polish authorities to leave Poland, Brother Daniel declared that he wanted to move to Israel because he was a Jew and had always wanted to live in the land of his fathers. His request to leave Poland was granted only after he forfeited his Polish citizenship, and he emigrated to Israel.

Upon arrival in Israel, Brother Daniel applied for a new immigrant's certificate, the right of every Jew coming to Israel, to enable him to become a permanent resident and a citizen. He asked to be registered as a Jew on his identity card. The Israeli authorities rejected his request. The then-minister of the interior, Socialist Israel Bar-Yehuda, wrote him a letter expressive of the dissent within the government itself: "Speaking for myself, I feel you have every right to be recognized as a Jew. However, I cannot award you the requested document because the government has reached a decision according to which a person cannot be registered as a Jew unless he declares unwittingly and without foreknowledge that he is a Jew and is not affiliated to any other religion."[13]

Bar-Yehuda's discomfiture at the decision that had been forced upon him was apparent. He ended the letter with justifications and expressed the hope that the government directive would actually be canceled and that he, as a minister in the cabinet, would be instrumental in achieving this.

Brother Daniel appealed to the Supreme Court against the decision of the minister of the interior. His main line of defense was the letter from the minister who, in principle, had supported him. But the wording of the Law of Return made the probability of his success negligible.

Section 2 of the law (in its original form) stated that every Jew had the right to immigrate to Israel. Section 3 (A) of same law determined that a Jew coming to Israel and expressing his desire to settle there would be issued a new immigrant identity card upon fulfilling three conditions:

1. He is a Jew (in the meaning of the word as defined in the body of the law).

2. He has come to Israel.

3. He has expressed a desire to settle in Israel.

The government's decisions and the directives of the minister of the interior reduced the scope of the Law of Return by stating that it would not be applicable to Jews who had converted to "another religion."

Brother Daniel made four points in his appeal:

1. The term "nationality" is not synonymous with the term "religion"—i.e., the nationality of a Jew is not auto-

matically synonymous with his religion.

2. In accordance with the halacha, in fact, he would be considered a Jew, as he was born of a Jewish mother.

3. The government decision upon which the minister of the interior based his refusal had no legal standing.

4. The minister's refusal was arbitrary and deviated from the framework of the law since it was based on extralegal considerations.

The appeal occupied the Supreme Court for nine months in 1962, with five justices presiding. The application was finally rejected by a majority decision, the latter written by Justice Dr. Moshe Silberg. It was a wide dissertation, and it was doubtful if it was entirely relevant to the judicial issue under discussion. The majority decision dealt with the halachic outlook, according to which the rule of law for a Jew is totally destroyed except for a few marginal rulings that have no real bearing on the principal issue.

Jewishness is a state of being, and this cannot be divided. The essence of Judaism, like that of all religions, is absolute: One is either Jewish or not Jewish. The condition is exclusive, and does not permit approximation or degrees of affiliation.

This is not so, however, with the Law of Return. It is a secular law and as such requires appropriate definition. The Law of Return is an original Israeli law, and not a transmutation of a British Mandate law. It is therefore logical that the term *Jew* should be defined according to Jewish understanding of its content and essence.

In fact, according to the everyday usage of the Jewish public, a Jew who has converted is not called a Jew. He is accepted as a Jew, but he is called a convert.

The legal ruling, however, specified that the State of Israel is not a theocratic state in which religion controls the life of its citizens. The court therefore cannot adopt the Orthodox—

i.e., standard religious—definition of the term *Jew*.

The court debated this problem at length, and emphasized that if it were guided by religious considerations, Brother Daniel would have won his lawsuit. But the court relied on the accepted view among ordinary people, for whom the terms *Jew* and *Christian* are mutually contradictory. In addition, as far as the ordinary understanding is concerned, a convert is not regarded as being part of the Jewish people. He has entered the fold, and hence is affiliated with it, but he has not been born into it.

Justice Silberg proposed that Brother Daniel be registerd as having no nationality, since according to Silberg's criteria, Brother Daniel was not a Jew in the secular definition demanded by the Law of Return. Concomitantly, he was not Polish, because he had renounced his Polish citizenship and nationality by emigrating from Poland to Israel.

By this conclusion, however, Justice Silberg created a legal ambiguity. In dealing with nationality, the same (Israeli) judicial system that recognizes renunciation of nationality and citizenship as being identical should likewise equate citizenship and nationality for purposes of being a Jew, and this patently was not so.

In addition, as far as the Polish authorities were concerned, all Jewish emigrants were regarded as identical. Ruffeisen received the same travel documents as others leaving from Poland for Israel. To Poland, the sole reason Ruffeisen was permitted to emigrate was his Jewishness.

The implicit contradiction between the court's decision and that of the government is only too obvious.

The government decision of July 20, 1958, placed a religious limitation on the term *Jew*. A person would be considered a Jew not in the secular sense of nationality but rather in a religious sense, albeit negative—a person was a Jew so long as he or she was not affiliated with any other religion.

The court decision in essence approved that Jewish nationality should be part of Jewish religiosity, ignoring the standard secular-polycentric understanding. This created the impression that the majority decision and Justice Silberg's reasoning were in fact cover-ups for the religious understanding of the word—despite the standard attitude that Israel is not a theocratic state and that religion does not rule the life of its citizens.

Even assuming that Christianity contradicts Jewish nationality, then why doesn't Polish, German, or Russian nationality contradict the essence of Jewish nationality? Nationality, after all, at least in the eyes of the man in the street and according to the court decision, is identified with anti-Semitism, persecution of Jews, and cultural persecution.

If the logic of the man in the street is accepted as the criterion determining the definition of Jewishness, could one then say that a Polish individual, who is Jewish insofar as he has never changed his religion, is not in fact a Jew? And what about all the Jews who, although they did not change their religion, denied their Jewishness—*not* at the time of the Holocaust, but only because it was more convenient? Would they be considered Jewish by the man in the street on whom Justice Silberg relied for his argument?

Is it possible, therefore, that the French socialist Prime Ministers Leon Blum and Pierre Mendes France would be considered Jews by nationality? It is doubtful that these men wanted this, even though they lit Sabbath candles in their homes. And where does Bruno Kreiski fit in, whose Jewish origin is unquestionable and whose Jewish brother lives in Jerusalem? Kreiski never converted, although the man in the street undoubtedly sees him as an "apostate to anger"! And what of those Jews who were drawn into Oriental sects? Is the poet Allen Ginsberg, a self-confessed follower of Buddhism, a Jew? And what of the Jews who by demonstration and declaration abandoned their Jewish religious belief and their Jewish national identity in order to bear the standard of communism, which denies both Talmudic tradition and religious belief, not to mention Zionism? In effect, by following the line of thought of the man in the street, Justice Silberg did no more than express an outlook of isolation and diminution that controls the Zionist religious camp. These "simple folk" whose view Justice Silberg expressed are apparently the Orthodox synagogue-goers who were weaned on hatred of outsiders and hatred of different views, and who deliberately and specifically absorbed the reasoning of excommunication implicit in the halacha toward apostates as well as toward unconventional thinkers and philosophers like Baruch Spinoza.

Knesset member Shulamit Aloni described this reasoning in biting words:[14]

> The NRP institution began taking care of the purity of the nation. A system of internal spying and tale bearing was developed, including through old community records; and anyone who was not a "kosher" Jew according to the halacha was put on the blacklist of people not qualified for [kosher] marriage. The lists increased, and so did the safety deposit boxes of the NRP. . . . At the outset, when the listing had just begun, it was recognized that the Israeli people would not accept this state of affairs, and so it was all kept secret. Zerach Warhaftig, then minister of religious affairs, even denied in the Knesset plenum the existence of those lists. After that statement, Mrs. Golda Meir said that the very thought frightened her. From the time the computerized lists

were found and made public, no one has been brought to trial. Rather the opposite has occurred—they have been legitimized. . . . This was based on the 1970 amendment, meantime accepted, of the Law of Return.

Thus, by automatic ruling, the judicial authorization given the Supreme Court to abrogate the Jewishness of any convert legitimized a witch hunt. It could be said that the reasoning of the government ruling is crypto-Orthodox.

An Italian columnist, writing immediately after the Ruffeisen ruling, claimed that Justice Silberg exchanged a religious criterion for a racist criterion, and that the test for rational thought was exchanged for the opinion of the man in the street.[15]

All in all, the Brother Daniel case had a dramatic influence on Jewish Orthodox radicalization.

In the short term, the Brother Daniel case and the reasoning of the majority of the bench unwittingly accelerated the radical process, which had already begun in the religious Orthodox camps in Israel as well as in the Diaspora. Opposed to the "statistical understanding" of so-called secular Judaism was the statistical understanding of the religious Orthodox. Their followers discovered and revealed that of fifty people to whom Ben Gurion had turned for their opinion on the essential meaning of the term *Jew,* only three had responded according to secular criteria. The remainder adhered to the criterion followed by the Orthodox.

The issue was in part psychological. The Orthodox claimed that the three "secular" opinions came from Judge Haim Cohen, author Haim Hazaz, and French psychiatrist Henri Bloch. In a convincing attempt to minimize the importance of these opinions, Dr. Ya'acov Meron presented the argument that Bloch was "the son of a woman who was Christian; he himself was married to a Christian."[16] As for Justice Haim Cohen, who had been ordained to the rabbinate at the Hebron yeshiva and was one of the spiritual and intellectual giants of modern Israel, according to Meron, he was "only Judge Cohen."

Meron's classification of protagonists and antagonists did not necessarily follow refined logic. For example, the name of Professor Yehoshua Heschel, the well-known Jewish theologian, was missing from among those who did not identify with the Orthodox definition of a Jew.[17] Heschel proposed an alternative definition according to which the State of Israel would recognize two kinds of terminology: (1) *Jewish,* for the person who regards himself as such also according to the religious criterion; and (2) *Hebrew,* for the person whose "genealogy" is national only.

As already noted, the extremists were the first to show tangible gains. In January 1965, the IDF refused to induct young Yael Zelbiri. Yael was born to a Jewish father and a Christian mother of Hungarian origin and had been baptized as a child. The population registry identified her as Christian by religion and Hungarian by nationality, thus automatically disqualifying her for the Israel Defense Forces.

To the non-Israeli reader this may appear to be a small loss. Why should Yael regret losing two years of her life to military service? This does not hold in Israel. Military discharge papers are essential to everyday living in Israel. They are a prerequisite for everything, from employment to higher education to social acceptance. Except for religious women who are exempt from military service, anyone not drafted into the IDF is automatically almost a pariah—the person is regarded as ill, or psychologically unbalanced, and unfit for life.

The establishment thus created a new category of misfits—the Israeli of "mixed" origin, having a Jewish father and a Gentile mother, and who was therefore regarded by society as inferior. Far from a preferred status, Yael and her parents looked upon her disqualification from military service as discrimination. The Jewish people are all too aware of the impact of discrimination. It creates a sense of alienation and inadequacy. This unspoken but very real pressure affected young Yael, who came to the conclusion that she was unwanted in Israel.

Justice Silberg was eventually to admit that neither a gradual awareness of the dangers posed by a theocracy nor an aversion to rabbinical rule guided him in his definition of "who is a Jew."

Shalit, Israeli Army Officer— a Jew Whose Son Is Not Jewish Enough

Four years after the case of Brother Daniel, Justice Silberg had the opportunity again to express his point of view. This time he did it openly and publicly, and no one could accuse him of hypocrisy.

The incident was the celebrated and unusual Shalit case.

The bench was made up of nine justices, led by Supreme Court Chief Justice Shimon Agranat. It was 1968, the year after the great victory of the Six Day War. Major Benjamin Shalit was an officer of the Israeli Army, and national fervor was at its height. Major Shalit, a Jew, was married to a nonaffiliated Gentile who regarded her personal fate and that of the State of Israel as inextricably interwoven. Their children were educated in Israel in the spirit of Israel-Jewish culture.

Despite the mother's religious origin, the children were registered as being of Jewish nationality with no religious affiliation, much as in the case of Ilana Stern.

With the new and militant wind blowing from the government benches, the minister Moshe Haim Shapiro (now in charge of the Ministry of the Interior) deliberately put his own personal view and that of his party, the NRP, to the test. The Shalit children were refused the status of being Jews by nationality. Major Shalit appealed to the Supreme Court against this verdict.

The minister of religious affairs based his verdict on two criteria: (a) the person will not be recognized as a Jew unless he/she is the son/daughter of a Jewish mother and he/she is not affiliated to any other religion; (b) if the person is not a Jew by virtue of having been born of a Jewish mother, he/she is not regarded as a Jew unless converted "properly" and not affiliated to another religion. The Ministry of the Interior declared that this definition "encompasses the norms of Jewish nationality and religion as one unit, and therefore a person cannot be regarded as Jewish by nationality if the Jewish religion does not see him/her as a Jew." According to this definition, the Shalit children could not be registered as Jews by nationality.

Justice Silberg, acting as deputy chief justice, delivered the minority opinion: "The problem, in all its implications, is: what is the content of the term 'Jew.' Can a person be affiliated with the Jewish people [nation], without at the same time also being of the Jewish religion? . . . Is there a criterion other than that of the halacha for determining the national identity of a Jew?"[18] It was thus that Justice Silberg expressed his understanding of Jewish nationality—that the religious criterion was nothing but Orthodoxy. At the time, it was a daring statement.

Finally, majority opinion ruled in favor of Shalit's appeal, as in the case of Ilana Stern. His children were registered as being Jewish by nationality.

However, the Ministry of the Interior produced yet another challenge—this time in terms of the 1970 amendment to the Law of Return. The amendment provided that it was not enough for a Jew to pass the religious criterion, he or she also had to fulfill the stricter addendum of "not being affiliated with another religion."

Eileen Dorflinger, an American Jew living in Israel, found that her Jewishness was in question.[19] She was a Jew who believed in Jesus, followed a messianic theology, and had been baptized according to Christian ritual. The last immediately put her beyond the pale.

But what of the Jew who believes in Jesus and the messianic theology, yet who has *not* been baptized? Is this individual a Jew in terms of the Law of Return? Should the decision be that a Jew ceases to be a Jew not necessarily by conversion but merely by so-called heretical belief? Should this happen, the Jewish people would face a rift even greater than the historic schism caused by the Karaite Jews.

In the Shalit case, Justice Bernson's judgment became a classic of its kind in demonstrating the widening rift between Orthodox isolation and renascent Jewish nationalism.

The verdict on the Shalit children was used as a pretext to force a government coalition crisis. Both Ministers Shapiro and Yosef Burg, of the NRP, demanded that the government bring an amendment to the law, which would invalidate the verdict on the Shalit children. The government faced with this dilemma was the first national unity government, led by Golda Meir but also bolstered by the Herut and Liberal parties led by Menachem Begin.

The new definition proposed that the spouse of a Jew,

and the descendants of a Jew, even if not from a Jewish mother, in actuality had never changed their religion. The second provision of the amendment defined the term *Jew* with painful precision, stating that a Jew is a person born of a Jewish mother and not affiliated with any other religion, or who has converted (to Judaism).

The second provision won the day, and the degradation of the Supreme Court was complete. On January 29, 1970, a Supreme Court decision was nullified by the Knesset.[20] The legislature had placed itself above the judiciary. The end result could be anticipated—segregation and national radicalization would from now on receive increasing support from the religious Orthodox camp. Few people, however, saw the writing on the wall. One of them was the Hebrew daily *Ha'Aretz,* which published a news item preceding the government's decision with the following headline: "The Israeli Government Is Being Drawn into a Dangerous and Terrifying Atmosphere. . . ."[21]

At the time, three years before the tragic Yom Kippur War, the members of the Mapam and Independent Liberal parties still had not fully realized that their political future was dimming and that being the antithesis of the NRP would in fact strengthen them. To the contrary—when the amended bill was tabled, Yitzhak Golan of the Independent Liberals abstained. He continued to do so without understanding that in certain issues abstention is equivalent to surrender.

The non-Orthodox Israeli public realized that something serious was at stake, and shook itself from its torpor. On February 10, 1970, a massive demonstration was held in the plaza fronting the Knesset. It was the second largest public demonstration seen in Israel until that time. (The largest was the demonstration organized in the fifties by Menachem Begin against accepting German reparations.) The brunt of the

organization was borne by the League Against Religious Coercion, although members of the Hashomer Ha'Tzair kibbutzim also played an active role.

However, the non-Orthodox religious Jews in Israel were
perturbed. They refused to sanction, let alone support, the
protest, leaving the demonstration emasculated in terms of
active change. The political establishment had won once again.

It is worthwhile examining the purpose and meaning of
the so-called less rigid group that constituted the screen hiding
clerical fanaticism.

The law specifically withholds the privilege of immigrating
to Israel as a Jew from any person born of a Gentile mother.
According to Orthodox reasoning, this means that person
is not a Jew. Children of Jewish fathers according to law
are permitted to settle in Israel although, also according to
law, *not* as Jews.

This was a heavy blow to Zionist reasoning, according
to which the State of Israel provides shelter for all those
who have suffered because they were Jews by returning to
them their honor as Jews.

The new law turned them into aliens in their own country.
They had a sort of special status as children who suffered
for the sins of their parents—they were children of mixed
ethnic origin because their mothers were not Jewish. The
absurdity of the law was clear, although it is doubtful if its
proponents had really examined it previously in this light.

Brother Daniel was the son of a Jewish mother. He also
was a Holocaust survivor who had remained a Jew throughout
the Holocaust. But his nationality was not recognized as Jewish
because of his conversion to Christianity. However, the provision of the law pertaining to children of mixed origin did
not hold for him because he was a Jew according to the
halacha and had converted according to his own free will.

On the other hand, consider the case of a Christian priest, the son of a Jewish father who converted to Christianity and who himself was baptized as an infant. The new law permits him legally to settle in Israel, and he is privileged to enjoy the rights refused to Brother Daniel, who was born a Jew.

Under the new law, Ilana Stern, nonreligious but the daughter of a Jewish father, would not be able to register her nationality as Jewish.

Let us use a hypothetical example: A new settler comes to Israel. His father was a Moslem by birth and his grandfather a Moslem by force of the Islamic faith. The religious lineage of the grandfather passes down to son and grandson. The settler's mother, however, was Jewish. Therefore, according to the criterion of the new law, the settler, even though a third-generation Moslem, is for legal purposes a Jew.

The new law created a new concept. Jewish nationality could no longer be acquired other than by a religious ceremony.[22]

Here is another example: A man who is the son of a Jewish father, educated at a Jewish school, a soldier in the IDF, and a Jewish patriot will not be recognized as a Jew unless he converts, nor will he be able to marry in Israel if his conversion does not satisfy the requirements of the Orthodox rabbinate. Should his philosophy be secular and should he be determined to retain his personal integrity and conscience and not acquire his Jewishness by undergoing a religious ceremony, he will never be considered a Jew. With luck, while performing a non-Orthodox conversion, he may be able to be registered as being a Jew (by religion and by nationality as well), but only as far as the Israeli citizenship (according to the Law of Return) is concerned.[23] Then, too, should he after all decide to marry a Jewish woman in Israel, an Orthodox conversion will be required. But it would be difficult to accept him as a neophyte, because the Gemara states that "anyone who converts for a woman, or for love, or from fear, is not a convert." Last but not least in this hypothetical case, the conversion process, which is also a naturalization process for the State of Israel, is a religious ceremony obliging a religious act. It would be hypocritical to ignore this aspect.

Conversion according to the halacha demands three essentials: ritual bathing, circumcision for males, and accepting and following the Jewish religious Commandments.

But people converted under duress, and who live in Hashomer HaTsair kibbutzim, face a dual issue. Their philosophy of Judaism is secular, that is, socialist. Their way of life on the kibbutz will not, of course, enable them to "keep the practical Commandments." Even more, the rabbinical-Orthodox order will be for them to move to an Orthodox neighborhood to enable them to fulfill the injuction that a convert should observe the religious Commandments.[24]

Is this the land Herzl envisaged? Was this the intention of the secular legislators in the Knesset? For all we know, this may merely be another step in the day-to-day pattern of security services and police activities, because the conversion procedure gives the rabbis a significant role in the practice of sovereign government.[25]

Israeli citizenship has a distinct pecking order. At the top of the ladder are the Jews whose mothers' Judaism is indisputable and whose name does not appear on the Ministry of Religion's blacklist. Next in line are children of parents who married a second time at a non-Orthodox ceremony, thus making the children suspect of being *mamzerim* (bastards in the Orthodox sense); Karaite Jews who are regarded as mamzerim or possible mamzerim; Cohens—members of the priestly tribe—who married divorcees; Ethiopian Jews and others whose observance is suspect; and many other such deviants from the rigid norm of the elite.[26]

Anyone slipping into the bastion of Judaism through a side door by converting under the aegis of a non-Orthodox rabbi places himself and all his descendants at risk of being considered goyim, or Gentile. While he will be registered as a Jew in the population registry, his name simultaneously will appear on the blacklist of the Ministry of Religion so as to prevent any denial of his doubtful status before the Israeli rabbinical tribunals that have exclusive control of all aspects of marriage and divorce. Even people who were registered as "pure" Jews before the change have not really crossed the barrier. Their children will face the test anew.

The entire scene is permeated by a sense of "Catch 22." Any man who is not a "pure" Jew, let alone an acknowledged Gentile, is forbidden to marry a "kosher" Jewish woman in Israel. He may of course marry her outside the borders of the State, but even that will not solve the problem for her children. The mother's marriage to a "doubtful" Jew affects her children, who in their turn will not be included in the select category unless they convert before the rabbinate. Even that, however, leaves them with the stain of having converted not from a pure heart but simply for convenience.

In addition, the new amendment has interesting side effects.

Since the rabbinical tribunal controls the status of nationality, it has a special relationship with the intelligence service and the police. In 1970, Chief Sephardic Rabbi Nissim revealed that the conversion process frequently is drawn out not only owing to ritual requirements but also because of the requirements of state security. He stated, "Of course, in any case conversion is not performed before receiving the results of the investigation of the Security Service and the police."[27]

The state's subordination to a single theological philosophy is almost total. Adjudication of personal affairs is completely under the control of the rabbinate. Even the act of naturalization—in all Western countries the prerogative of the state—is subject in Israel to the permission of religious authorities.

Some loopholes, however, still remain. For example, according to the present amendment, conversion may be performed according to Orthodox, Reform, or Conservative ritual.[28] The Jewish religious-Orthodox establishment still has to take care of a few tag ends in order to eliminate from the definition in the Law of Return the last remnants of its secular origin. Once done, this will very soon establish a single entrance to Judaism—via Orthodox conversion. The target should be achieved quite easily, as the entire Likud bloc now supports the demands of the Orthodox on this issue.

When Rabbi Nissim was asked during the debate on the amendment to the Law of Return whether a Reform conversion would be acceptable to the rabbinate, his response was lukewarm. He had no personal opinion on the subject, he said, while the Chief Rabbinate had not yet discussed the matter, and it all depended on the wording of the law. He did not amplify this vague comment.

Before the vote was taken, the Knesset remained low-key as well. A number of Labor members also approved the amendment. One Knesset member, the late Mordechai Zar, declared that it was not that anyone who felt like it could simply declare himself a Jew. Knesset member Gad Ya'acobi gave an answer more characteristic of his party. He was not in favor of the legislation, he said, but he was in favor of party discipline, and the topic was not only philosophical but also political. Knesset member Shalom Levin, general secretary of the Teachers Union and also ambitious in the field of public-secular education, said that if the government could withstand a crisis, he would consider voting with his party. In the event, the only solid political stance opposing the religious legislation came from the groups to the left of Labor.

The argument over the definition of a Jew was seen, at best, as a struggle between the secular groups and the religious establishment. Politicians affiliated to the various secular parties and who incline toward the traditional view of Judaism were ambivalent about the change. Politicians who saw continuation of Labor rule as beneficial to the State regarded acquiescence in the demands of the religious parties as reasonable—this was the only means of preserving that rule.

Cold logic dictated the need to preserve the "historic covenant" between religious Zionist Orthodoxy and the ruling Labor Party in the Histadrut (the general workers union) and in the settlements. This meant, in their own words, "not exaggerating" the intrinsic worth of the concession. After all, any intelligent person well knew that in any case religious Orthodoxy rules Israel in all matters regarding anything to do with the personal aspect of Jewishness, so a change in the Law of Return and the Population Registry Act was not particularly significant. This was a hard reality that had been established during previous concessions, regardless of whether it was the Rabbinical Tribunals Act of 1953, which laid down rules for marriage and divorce; the transfer of authority over the budget for religious institutions to the religious councils; or the maintenance of legislation regulating Sabbath observance, kashrut, or public transport according to Orthodox demands.

The NRP, "Good Shepherd" of True Jewishness

The NRP found it appropriate to assist the Labor Party in crystallizing public awareness of the change so as to reduce the impact of opposition that in any case did not derive from above and consistently lacked the required financial means and organization to carry out its purpose.

The real victory of the NRP was the agreement of the establishment to the Orthodox claim that this was a struggle between the secular and the religious, and that Jewish secularism was only the result of the formal existence of a Jewish state—a kind of wild growth in the overall landscape of the Jewish world. The argument went that, except for the oppressed Jews of the Soviet Union, world Jewry is religious and the NRP is its spokesman.

The NRP argued further that the amendment was required for the sake of a whole nation, a whole Jewish tradition, and the wholeness of the Torah of Israel. It gave as proof that religious groups in the United States also demanded the amendment. (No one noticed that these groups were for the most part in the Orthodox minority.)

Non-Orthodox religious Jewry stood on the sidelines, not really understanding why it should participate in the wars of the Jews. Claims such as those of religious coercion made by the Orthodox establishment against the secular majority in Israel would never be made by American citizens, nor would Americans become involved in or identify with them. These were the internal affairs of a sovereign state with democratically elected institutions.

American Jews who are not Zionists are not interested in internal Zionist squabbles. Those who are Zionists but not Orthodox fear for the future sovereignty of the young state. Their role is limited to financial aid and assistance, as far as possible, on the international scene—in short, to help, but not to get involved in controversial issues, particularly when this involvement might cause a schism in Diaspora Jewry and thus prevent unified action when necessary. Both the Jewish Agency establishment and the bureaucracy of the Israeli Foreign Ministry took this stand and enhanced it with their prestige. Who, after all, would question the wisdom emanating from Jerusalem?

The non-Orthodox religious movements read the writing on the wall only too well. However, by their own definition they were ambivalent and did not take sides. This religious leaning was not totally rejected by the Reform and Conservative movements. They may not be Orthodox, but they are Jewish and religious, and so long as there is mutual respect between the Reform and Conservative majority and the Orthodox minority in the United States, the same mutual respect will be maintained in Israel.

To American Jews, the fact that marriages and divorces are under the control of the Orthodox doesn't really matter. Politicians of the first rank have said no one need worry because Reform Jews will immigrate in large numbers, and the Orthodoxy may compromise.

What of the Conservatives? In their heart of hearts they hoped to get along with the Orthodox establishment, and perhaps have its help integrating into Israel's religious establishment.

But the Reform Jews, too, who came to Israel and cried havoc about the construction of the Archaeological Institute to camouflage the activities of the Hebrew Union College, took a position of self-protection. At first, they were attacked with the utmost insolence. They were accused of carrying out mixed marriages, of being ignorant in matters of halacha, of being responsible for apostasy, of leading the public astray, and generally of being a catastrophe for the people of Israel. The small group of Reform Jews who established themselves in Israel tried to defend themselves against such charges. Their position wasn't strengthened by the fact that most of them were Americans. In a ludicrous attempt to placate the Orthodox, they began wearing yarmulkes. The Orthodox, for once absolutely correct, were disgusted by the transparent maneuver, while the secular public did not understand the Reform Jews and did not see them as allies in the struggle. Although several Reform rabbis joined the more militant movements, the representative Reform body remained aloof. They were mildly afraid of the Reform movement being tagged as secular. This trend within the Reform movement in Israel changed, however, when a new, Israeli-born generation of Reform leaders began to exercise more militant positions, joining other liberal groups.

The issue of separating religion and nationality in any case did not involve the non-Orthodox. There seemed no point in becoming tangled in it because they didn't see it as their war. As long as the clash didn't cut too deeply they remained in the camp. The non-Orthodox hadn't considered that to hurt one was to hurt all. The general public feeling in Israel was one of hopeless confusion, as was that of the secular political establishment. The non-Orthodox religious movements stood by, onlookers to a vicious struggle and oblivious to the fact that it was taking place in their own home.

The preservation of pluralism in Judaism, the reflection of the different concepts, and the understanding of Judaism as an expression of both the national and religious reality were all pushed aside. Everyone preferred to play it safe and wait. This enabled Menachem Begin on February 9, 1970, to make a deliberate and calculated statement in the Knesset in favor of the change. With great emotion he asked the rabbis to "facilitate conversion." No one took much note of the injury done and offense caused to Reform and Conservative Judaism.

The underlying message of Begin's statement was that the confrontation was really between the false prophet of secular nationalism and the gallant Orthodox out to prevent intermarriage and thus save the nation from some terrible admixture of impurity.

The amendment was not totally opposed by the Labor Party, whose members dutifully followed coalition discipline and voted in favor. In the Liberal camp there was more hesitation, especially from the Pinchas Rosen school. But Yitzhak Arzi, who would later lead the party, was not alone in applauding the amendment.[29]

The Dualities—Rabbinical and Civil, Orthodox and Non-Orthodox

During those bleak winter days of 1970, the weather matched the political tone. The prestigious Hebrew-language daily *Ha'Aretz* ran an article headlined "There Is No Real Opposition to Religious Domination":

> For many years David Ben-Gurion tried to build the state on the principle that Israel is a state of law and not a state of halacha. All his, and our, compromises with the religious groups did not really harm this principle, but the new law . . . determines that the most basic issues, those of religion and nationality, are determined according to halacha.
>
> From now on the question is, if such a fundamental matter is decided according to the halacha,

why shouldn't other matters, which are much more superficial, also be determined according to the halacha?[30]

When the smoke of battle cleared, the true picture emerged.

The Orthodox religious camp, headed by the NRP, have always systematically acted to delegitimize the Jewish and universal values that are not very visible but nevertheless an intrinsic part of secular, sovereign Zionism. With infinitely more practical impact, they also set out to exchange them for what they call "historical Jewish" values—the fossilized values of rabbinical Orthodox halacha.[31]

The great usurption of words, terms, and concepts began.

Upon the establishment of the State of Israel, the religious polity lost the terms *Israel* and *Israeli*. From then on they were in the secular domain and defined the state and the citizenship of its subjects, both Jewish and non-Jewish. They no longer expressed the religion of Israel but the new sovereignty, the new state.

This is the source of the furor surrounding the word *Jewish*. Its original use was as an expression to define the renascent nationality in our land. This is the source, too, of the furor over the word *Hebrew*—the word that Ben-Gurion loved, and that the Hebrew youth embraced, so that the Hebrew army took root alongside the Hebrew language.

The Hebrew court is not the sovereign court but in fact the rabbinical court or tribunal. It is the Talmudic court from which the term "Jewish values" was usurped, rather as if those values emanate only from the Talmudic schools of learning.

The struggle to establish Orthodox halacha by virtue of the sovereign state of Israel delegitimized the entire regime. State courts were matched by parallel rabbinical courts. Local government systems were matched by parallel regional religious councils. Public secular education was matched by parallel public religious and independent haredi education. The law on women's rights was matched by even more powerful religious laws preventing a woman from being an equal witness in the full legal sense of this term.

Court judges who declared their loyalty to the State of Israel and its laws were matched by religious *dayanim*— judges—who do *not* declare their loyalty to the laws of the State of Israel even though they hold their appointment by grace of those laws.

The sovereign legislative body, the Knesset, was matched by a strengthened Chief Rabbinate, which acts by force of law while emphasizing its independence. It even resents the rare occasions when in theory it is superseded by the Supreme Court sitting as the High Court of Justice.

In effect, the religious-Orthodox establishment succeeded in reducing Israel's sovereign status by reverting to a situation matched under Ottoman rule, when the Turkish Postal Service was paralleled by French, Russian, and Austrian postal services competing with the sovereign postal service. Those foreign consuls further eroded the already diminishing power of Turkish sovereignty.

Justice Silberg bluntly expressed the accepted reasoning of the Orthodox public when, during the Shalit case, he rhetorically asked: "Is there any criterion other than that of the halacha for determining the national identity of a Jew?"

When this halachic criterion was authorized as a criterion of the sovereign Knesset, the State was annexed to the Orthodox establishment, losing any association between what it was and what it had been hoped to be. The Zionist "secular" laws were emasculated.

With secular nationalism having lost its legitimacy, the Labor Party could do nothing but make the best of things by adjusting and amending until the state's authority resembled a crazy patchwork quilt. It seemed that at every opportunity Orthodoxy was strengthened at the expense of state sovereignty.

The Labor Party could only hope that it would not be dragged into the extremist vortex, while the Orthodox camp in its turn leaned heavily toward extremism to catch up and overtake the Labor party, and also to demonstrate in it an absence of leadership.

Neither the leaders nor the grassroots membership of the Labor party absorbed the full significance of the change. When the founders of the democratic, pluralistic government conceded to the demands of the religious Orthodox, and relinquished authority to the Orthodox, the Labor party had nothing to offer in its stead. The NRP had been a very effective Trojan horse.

On coming to power, the Likud bloc introduced and highlighted nationalism, and the ultra-Orthodox proved to so-called "moderate" religious-Orthodox Zionism that Orthodoxy in the State of Israel need not necessarily be Zionist.

The state of the Jews was dead: long live the Jewish state!

Now came the turn of the Jewish community in the free world. When the State of Israel rallied around religious Orthodoxy, it did not bear in mind the danger to the unity of the Jewish people. Israel has such a strong influence on world Jewry that by delegitimizing non-Orthodoxy within its own body politic, it simultaneously delegitimized non-Orthodox leadership in the Diaspora.

The time had come to make an additional amendment to the Law of Return. But this time it was not a clash between religious and secular; rather, the battle raged inside the Jewish religion. The Orthodox camps in Israel wanted to consolidate their hegemony and to let world Jewry know just who held the reins. At the very least, the final sanction of non-Orthodox authority over their followers would lie with the Orthodox establishment in Israel.

This time, the leaders of U.S. Jewry had the knife pressed against their throats. Only now was it understood that from the outset the struggle had not been against the already cowed secular Jews—its real aim was uniform Orthodoxy.

The only winner so far in the conflict has been Orthodoxy. The opposition of secular Israelis has merely given the Orthodox further room for movement and attack against the other Jewish religious factions.

The real victim is Jewish history from the time of the emancipation at the turn of the century, through the Holocaust, and up to the establishment of the state of the Jews.

Political Zionism is the history of the emancipation and the yearning of the Jews for a definition as an independent nation. It became a part of the overall surge toward national identity that swept Europe at the turn of the century. The simultaneous development of modern Zionism and the struggle for independence in the fractionalized Austro-Hungarian empire is no coincidence.

Religious Jewish Orthodoxy stood on the sidelines. Not only did it not want to join in the fray, but it actively opposed the very concept.

The late Professor Benyamin Akzin wrote that the introduction to Israel's Declaration of Independence had the same motivation as the American Declaration of Independence. The introduction, said Professor Akzin, "goes to prove that the establishment of the State should be seen as justified because of the extraordinary past of the Jewish people and also because of the 'natural right . . . to be like any independent nation in its sovereign state.' "[32] The essence of this argument is that like all the nations the nation of Israel is a people that has a religion; it was never conceived as a religion that has a people.

The Holocaust is an indelible part of Israeli memory. When Hitler set out on his "final solution" for the Jews, it was he who decided who was a Jew and was therefore to be destroyed. The enlightened world, including the State of Israel, has accepted without any dissent that the six million who were annihilated *as* Jews indeed *were* Jews. They all were saints; they all merited eternal remembrance. Since the establishment of the modern state, Israel annually observes a special day to sanctify the memory of the six million martyrs.

Israel's Reparations Act ratified compensation from Konrad Adenauer's Federal Republic of Germany for the six million Jewish victims of the Nazi regime. The only opposition to this legislation came from Menachem Begin and Knesset member Dov Szylanski, later to be a deputy minister in Begin's government. They organized violent demonstrations against it, but neither they nor anyone else ever questioned the accuracy of the number of victims, nor their Jewishness.

The religious parties were stolidly silent. They didn't even murmur that, according to their own halachic definition of Jewishness, not all those six million victims were Jews. They never doubted the victims' Jewishness when a great forest planted in their memory covered the slopes of the hills of Jerusalem. They never doubted the sanctity of the holy ashes brought to Yad V'Shem, the brooding memorial to the six million set in the Jerusalem Forest. The mind sickens at the memory of this hypocritical silence.

When discussing the halachic definition of a Jew, the Orthodox often use the Hebrew term equal to *mischling* to denote a child of mixed origin. The identical term is used in the Nuremberg Laws.[33] Hitler held that a child of mixed origin is a Jew in any circumstances. The Orthodox hold that a child of mixed origin whose Jewishness is a patrilineal heritage is not a Jew.

As a matter of curiosity, an Orthodox Jewish prayer book reads in express patrilineal terms contradicting matrilineal Orthodox ruling: "Blessed art Thou, Lord our God and God of our fathers, God of Abraham, God of Isaac and God of Jacob. . . ."

The Nationality Act of the Third Reich as amended on November 14, 1935, states that a Jew is a person who has at least three Jewish grandparents. The amendment does not distinguish between male and female lineage. A mischling is someone who had at least two Jewish grandparents, again regardless of sex.

The Nuremberg Laws defined a member of the religious community as a person who married a Jew, male or female, after the enactment of the law, and who continued in that marriage.

Again, according to the Nuremberg Laws, a child born of a married couple of whom only one was Jewish, regardless of sex, was a Jew. A child born out of wedlock to parents of whom one was Jewish, regardless of sex, was a Jew.

Six million human beings died in searing agony, in the terrible suffocation of gas, in the gnawing pain of starvation, or simply and possibly worst, in complete loss of hope, solely because they were Jews. That, at least, was one point of total agreement between the Nazi overlords and their victims. Those six million were all Jews. They died as Jews, and they were killed as Jews.

The definition of a Jew in the Nuremberg Laws is distinct, sharp, and leaves no room for any doubt. The Orthodox definition also is distinct, sharp, and leaves no room for any doubt.

One can only conclude that the silence of the Orthodox camp about the number of victims of the Nazi Holocaust was a silence of consent. The logical sequel is that a person who sacrifices himself as a Jew, a person who suffered in the Nazi inferno as a Jew, and a person who was annihilated as a Jew, is not only a Jew, but a Jewish hero and martyr.

How is it, then, that the religious-Orthodox establishment, with all its so-called veneration for the Torah as the only source of law and halacha as the only kind of law, agreed with Hitler's legal definition of a Jew? Or, if they agreed with his broad definition of a Jew, why can they now not apply that same broad definition for living Jews?

It is nightmarish to record that a nation that suffered from selection, separation, and racism, has itself made statutory distinctions concerning Jews.

The religious Orthodoxy apparently learned nothing from the Holocaust, or at least nothing about the meaning of a common fate for Jews. In discussing his law of determinism, Jean-Paul Sartre mentioned the same issue.[34] The response of Orthodox Jewry was that it is not for the Gentiles to determine who is a Jew.

From a religious point of view, there may be some basis to this claim. But there is also a social and historical contradiction inherent in it: If the Gentiles are not to use persecution and murder to determine who is a Jew, why are other Gentiles condemned for causing the assimilation of Jews?

Hence historical determinism does have a certain significance, and religious Orthodoxy also falls prey to it. The secular camp in Israel also felt this historical pressure and, in fact, did not ask for anything other than the recognition of children of mixed origin as Jews.

Reform Judaism, whose thunderous silence in the seventies was helpful in the clericalization of Israel, has now adopted the outlook of the secular camp and recognized their common interest. Today, for the first time since the establishment of the State, there is agreement, virtually a covenant, between the needs of Jewish nationalism in Israel and those of Reform Jewry. The Holocaust and the founding of the State of Israel bridged the gulf that had previously existed and helped the secular and the religious Reform Israeli to find a common connection.

Orthodox Jewry is having difficulty dealing with the phenomenon of the establishment of the State of Israel as a corporeal, secular entity.

Religious Judaism sees the people of Israel and the law of Israel as one. The Orthodox interpretation of this philosophy is for the people of Israel to observe the Commandments of the divine law as an expression of their Jewishness, to be different from the Gentiles, and to be the Chosen People. Orthodoxy gives a dire warning against any attempt to be like other nations. It is this interpretation that gave rise in Orthodoxy to the popular aphorism that rather than Israel preserving the Sabbath, the Sabbath preserved Israel.

Because of these rigid commands, there is no room for compromise. In essence, we are creating a Jewish community that keeps the commandments for dietary ritual (kashrut) by prohibiting raising pigs and eating leavened bread on Passover, but does not ease the prohibition on travel and work on the Sabbath and on religious holidays.

It is also a commandment to enforce the observance of a commandment, as it is said: "Reprove your neighbor but do not incur guilt because of him."

The Orthodox understanding of the Sabbath, however, sharply contradicts the expressed aims of the State of Israel, which were outlined in the Declaration of Independence and in a series of fundamental decisions by the Supreme Court. There is no way this contradiction can be overcome.

The penetration of Orthodox values into the state ordinances necessarily forced the delegitimization of the values of tolerance, pluralism, and democracy as they are understood by free Western societies. Nothing can halt the process. Eventually it will forcibly turn the state of the Jews into a closed and isolated Jewish community that rejects any questioning and makes do with "hazarah b'teshuvah" (repentance).

Quite aside from the examples already given, the beginnings of this hardening of thought, this mental sclerosis, are already clearly visible.

Rabbi Eliezer Waldenberg, a dayan, or religious judge, who was awarded the Israel Prize for Jewish Thought in 1976, quotes halachic sources which teach that foreigners are not permitted to reside in Jerusalem. He has also prominently enunciated another halachic law that forbids foreigners to be in the majority among residents in the provincial towns of Israel.

It is difficult to avoid the feeling that recalling these halachic strictures and frequently pronouncing them in public creates fertile ground for extremist thought among the religious and even for putting these thoughts into action. We have already seen vivid examples of the result.

It is enough to recall that Knesset member Rabbi Meir Kahane attempted to table a bill with the following provisions: segregated beaches where it will be forbidden for Arabs and Jews to swim together; segregated apartment buildings where it will be forbidden for Arabs to live in the same apartments with Jews; and the restriction of Israeli citizenship to Jews.[35]

There is an inherent paradox here. Certain segments of the religious-Orthodox Zionist public are at present ready to join in the struggle against religious ultra-Orthodox coercion. This is due not to a sudden rush of tolerance but rather to a suspicion by the Zionist Orthodox that both the ultra-Orthodox and Kahane are snapping at their heels. The nationalist religious public is being pushed into an awkward position, with synagogues taken over and education channeled not only in a nationalistic direction but also in an ultra-Orthodox direction.

This suspicion, however, should not give rise to false hopes. While the Zionist Orthodox community is beginning to recognize the creeping shadow of the ultra-Orthodox, it is entering the fray to struggle not for tolerance as a general principle but only for tolerance for itself as a specific group.

To the contrary, however, the schism between various religious-Orthodox groups (including violent clashes between the different Hassidic dynasties) proves that the only defense for human rights and the only existing framework for the continuation of the Jewish community in Israel is a democratic, pluralistic state with tolerance as a cornerstone of its structure.

The Orthodox Jewish population can exist and develop in a state with precisely such liberal government because only this framework could support the extreme ideological sensitivity of these groups without their degenerating into violent conflict among themselves. Because of their own particular narrow character, however, no one Orthodox stream could preserve and lead a pluralistic, democratic rule.

Nonetheless, one cannot overlook the intricacy of Israel's social and legal makeup.

During the Shalit case Justice Bernson expressed his fear that a rabbinical Orthodox dictatorship would destroy Israel's national dimension. Here is a vivid illustration of that possibility. It is the real story of an Israeli family.

Israeli Children—Hebrew by Culture, But Not Jewish

In a provincial town in Argentina, a young Jew, a Zionist, met a Gentile Argentinian girl. For him, the place where they met was quite natural—the local Zionist-socialist club.[36] But what brought her there?

According to the girl, she had been deeply moved by the romanticism of an old-new nation renewing its sovereignty in the land of its forefathers, and had developed a growing identification with Israel.

The boy planned to emigrate to Israel, and she was happy to go with him. They married while still in Argentina where their first child was born and circumcised without any religious ceremony. He was given a Hebrew name.

The little family emigrated to Israel. Both husband and wife found jobs in the public service sector and settled down happily to their new life. Their second child, also a boy, was born in Israel.

Over the years, however, the marriage failed and the parents separated. Between themselves, they came to an agreement about the custody of the children. They would spend most of the week with their mother and the weekends with their father.

The wife suddenly decided to return to Argentina, claiming, quite reasonably, that it was difficult for her to live in Israel. Her absorption in Israel was only superficial, she said. As a Gentile, she found doors were closed to her advancement in the public service. Although there was no material evidence of this, it was undoubtedly a strong enough subjective feeling to motivate a crucial decision.

The divorce was agreed upon without any animosity, but then the fate of the children brought the matter before the Jerusalem District Court. The wife claimed that since she was not Jewish, neither were the children. In any case, she argued, Israel was not their homeland, because when they grew up the boys would suffer from discrimination. They would be alien in their surroundings because, being Gentiles, they would always wear the mark of Cain that branded them as different. Since Israeli law relating to personal status is religious, they also would not be able to raise a family in Israel because they were not affiliated to any particular religion.

Her assertion was unarguable. No institution in Israel would marry such people who, according to the halacha, are unfit for marriage.

The mother concluded, therefore, that the children would build happier lives in Argentina, and the sooner they embarked on that course, the better. As for the father, she maintained that if he did not want to be separated from the children and they really were important to him, he, a native Argentinian, should also return to his homeland.

The father, in turn, unequivocally refused to return to Argentina. He was a Jew, a Zionist, and his home was in Israel. It was illogical to uproot the children and take them off to another country simply because of the problems of one of the parents. The mother's particular problem would not affect the children for several years. By then the boys would be adults and there would no longer be any reason for a legal directive as to which parent they would live with.

The crux of the father's argument, however, was that the boys should strike roots in Israel precisely because their father was a Jew.

Professor Isaacson, a Jewish Argentinian historian, was brought as an expert witness. He testified that Argentinian society derives from Roman Catholic cultural sources, where everything associated with family structure relates to the father. Accordingly, the father's religion would decide that of the children and they would be identified as Jews. This aspect of the Roman Catholic faith is so strong that it was doubtful that their status as Jews would change even if they should convert to Christianity.

When the verdict finally was delivered, it centered on the issue of Israel as the children's heartland. The questions were sweeping: Were the children rooted in Israel? Were they in any way alienated? What was their language? What was their culture? What essentially was the happiest balance—letting them grow up in a familiar environment or dragging them off to a strange country?

The father's argument convinced the court, which ruled that the children should remain in Israel according to the terms of the agreement contracted between the parents before the case. If the mother preferred emigrating from Israel, that was her business, but she could not bind the children to a personal decision applying to herself.

The father asked the court to permit him to explain just why the children's mixed parentage was not a stain on their nationality, and that it certainly did not make them strangers in their homeland or deprive them of a personal identity.

He argued that separation of religion and nationality was appropriate to Herzl's principle of the "the state of the Jews." Applying the philosophy of Sartre, the father said that from a social standpoint a person is a Jew when his Gentile surroundings hold him to be a Jew.

This point was picked up by Professor Isaacson: "The liturgical aspect . . . according to which Christianity is received by baptism, is not reflected in the social sphere, since the son of a Jewish father always remains Jewish in the popular [non-Jewish] consciousness."

In 1964, Justice Haim Cohen had said, "If Hitler denied an individual the privilege of personally choosing whether or not to be Jewish, it is incumbent upon us, and not solely for this reason, to return this basic privilege to the individual." Arthur Ruppin, a Zionist leader before World War II, once said, "An individual is affiliated to the same nation, that is, to the same national community, with which he himself feels most closely associated—historically, linguistically, and culturally."[37]

In his argument that the boys should remain in Israel for their own future well-being and sense of personal security, Ruppin added, "The Nuremberg Laws returned to Judaism the children of mixed marriages."

The case of the Argentinian immigrants had been preceded in the sixties by similar cases, including that of Rina Eitani of Upper Nazareth. She was born to a Gentile mother and a Jewish father. The Ministry of the Interior asked Rina to return her passport so that her nationality "could be corrected."

Rina Eitani refused to accede to this request, and in the autumn of 1964 massive public demonstrations were held in her support. There is no better proof that, despite its ethnic diversity, the broad public in Israel accepts as Jews the children of a Jewish father, regardless of the non-Jewishness of the mother.

The court decision in the case of the Argentinian immigrants is important both because of the arguments given by the defense, and also because it emphasizes that even after the 1970 amendment to the Law of Return, there are still aspects of Israeli life that will be recognized despite the negative effect of the amendment. The most important of these is that people who fail the who-is-a-Jew test according to the Law of Return nevertheless may have an abiding attachment to Israel. Evidently the rabbinical tribunals, with their control of the personal status of Jews in Israel, have not succeeded in stifling human emotions.

In practice, an Israeli citizen's Jewishness is an important component of his life. It is legally expressed at four levels in which he cannot escape or ignore his religious affiliation and nationality, since nationality also is dictated by the religious criterion.

Laws of Citizenship, Population Registration, and the Law of Return

The 1970 amendment to the Law of Return[38] determines as follows with regard to children of mixed marriages:

> The privileges of a Jew according to this act, and the privileges of a new immigrant according to the Citizenship Act of 1952, and the privileges of a new immigrant according to any other legislation, are also given to the child and grandchild of a Jew, to the Jew's spouse, and to the spouse of the child and grandchild of a Jew, except for a Jew who voluntarily converted.
>
> It is not germane whether the Jew from whom the privilege [of being a Jew] comes down, as in subsection (a) above, is alive or deceased or whether or not he has immigrated to Israel.
>
> The restrictions and conditions determined for a Jewish immigrant in this act, or in accordance with this act, or in the legislation mentioned in subsection (a), will be incumbent upon any person who also requests the privilege according to subsection (a). (Article 4A[a])

With regard to the Jew, the 1970 amendment states: "For purposes of this act, a Jew is: 'a person born to a Jewish mother or one who converted to Judaism and who is not affiliated to any other religion.' " (Section 4B)

The legislature took a liberal approach, asking that identical material privileges be awarded to a child of mixed origin as to the recognized Jewish child. For the first time since World War II, however, the legislature of a democratic state apparently founded on the principle of equality among human beings, took measures to state definitively that children of mixed origin constitute a separate legal category.

The Rabbinical Tribunals

The 1953 Act for the Jurisdiction of Rabbinical Tribunals (Marriage and Divorce) placed marriage and divorce in the control of religious tribunals. Here the definition of a Jew is halachic-Orthodox without any reservations. Paradoxically, according to this definition and to the requirements of the rabbinical tribunals, both Brother Daniel and Eileen Dorflinger are Jewish, because the Talmud holds that "even if Israel has sinned, he is still Israel."

It follows, therefore, that a person cast out of the Jewish fold in terms of the Law of Return, because of having converted from Judaism, is still a Jew. Conversely, a person whose Judaism is irreproachable but who does not meet the harsh Talmudic criterion, will be denied Jewish status.

A Cohen—that is, someone descended from the priestly caste—is forbidden to marry a (female) convert or a divorcee.

The laws of leviratic marriage (*chalitza*) persecute the widowed sister-in-law of a man whose brother has died. She is put to strict and offensive tests in order to win the privilege of remarriage.

In several cases, and they are not very rare, the rabbinical tribunal permits a husband to take an additional wife. Thus criminal law in Israel allows Jews to practice bigamy when it has been permitted, with certain limitations, by the Chief Rabbinical Council.

In only the year 1984-85, seventy-six requests were approved in Israel to marry an additional wife. For the same period, in Jerusalem alone, eighteen such requests were granted.

Whenever these cases are publicized, the public briefly stirs in spontaneous reaction. Ruth Tekoa, chairwoman of the Women's International Zionist Organization, in Israel, used the opportunity presented by the publication of the 1984-85 statistics to condemn the practice whereby marriages authorized by the tribunal of the Orthodox Chief Rabbi "return it to the Dark Ages."

Unfortunately, experience has shown that the Orthodox establishment continues its practices undisturbed. Since the law under which the new marriages fall is the law of the Torah, a person will not be prosecuted according to Article 179 (prohibition of polygamy) if the new marriage was performed after he received permission to marry according to the judgment of the Rabbinical Tribunal and the judgment was authorized by the Chief Rabbi in his capacity as President of the High Rabbinical Tribunal.

For non-Jews the restrictions on polygamy are much more severe. Polygamy is permitted only in the following very rare instances: (a) If the spouse, owing to mental incapacity, is unable to agree to end the marriage by divorce, or to nullify it; (b) if the spouse from a previous marriage is absent due to argument; or (c) if the spouse from a previous marriage is missing under circumstances that raise sufficient apprehension for his or her life, and there has been no trace of the spouse for seven years. A by-product of these directives is that an Israeli citizen who is Moslem by religion, which permits him to follow a limited polygamous lifestyle with up to four wives, will only be permitted to take a second wife under severe restrictions. In this way, the Israeli legislature discriminates between the Israeli citizen who follows the Law of Moses and the Israeli citizen who is an adherent of Islam or Christianity.

Over and above all these instances, the present structure of the criminal law gives the Chief Rabbi in his capacity as President of the High Rabbinical Tribunal the authority to allow bigamy in a sweeping range of circumstances. For example, a case was reported in which the High Rabbinical Tribunal permitted a man to marry a second wife after his first wife developed epilepsy, even though her illness was medically authenticated as no longer being active.

In practice, the religious monopoly held by the Orthodox is emasculating civil law, which cannot withstand the Talmudic halacha that determines the laws governing the Jews.

The secular public was up in arms when the Law of Return was amended at the pleasure of the Orthodox groups. Nobody observed that the amendment was less novel than it seemed, since the Jewishness of the average Israeli comes daily under Talmudic scrutiny by virtue of the authority granted the rabbinical tribunals. They pronounce on fitness to marry, to become a national (after conversion inside Israel), and to be a registered marriage officer. These rabbis are not recognized if they are not affiliated with the Talmudic rabbinical Orthodox establishment.

The Ethiopian Jews are the most recent example of the decrease in sovereign state power and the increase in the power of Talmudic thinking, which is eroding the development of rule of law in Israel.[39]

When the dramatic Operation Moses to bring the Ethiopian Jews to Israel began in 1985, the Chief Rabbinate was faced with a new and potent challenge.

The Chief Rabbinate did not have the power to interfere directly with the registration of the new Ethiopian immigrants according to the Law of Return. It was state authorities who issued them Israeli citizenship documents recognizing their Judaism according to civil law (the Law of Return).

The Chief Rabbinate set up the obstacle in its own court. Any Jew who wants to marry has to appear before the marriage registry, which is under the jurisdiction of the Chief Rabbinate. There the Ethiopian Jew was told that a condition for marriage registration is that he undergo ritual bathing.

The rabbis had neglected the fact that the Ethiopian Jews, like the Jews of Europe, lived and survived for centuries under a Christian rule that enticed or persecuted them with the concept of baptism. For example, with the end of enlightened Western rule in Spain, the Catholic rulers gave Jews the humanitarian choice of baptism, fire, or expulsion. Most of the Spanish Jews either died in the flames of the Inquisition or were expelled. A few preferred to survive in Spain at the cost of converting to Christianity, although they remained Jews spiritually.

When Operation Moses brought 70 percent of all the Jews of Ethiopia to Israel it was regarded as the miracle of the eighties. A 3,000-year-old community had survived persecution and famine to come to the Promised Land.

In Ethiopia as well as Israel, and as in the Catholic Spain of Queen Isabella, the religious establishment controls central aspects of life. In Israel, the Ethiopians have been requested upon order of the Chief Rabbinate to undergo ritual immersion. If they don't, they will not be regarded as Jews for purposes of marriage registration, nor will they be able to raise families here. Yet, if they capitulate and undergo ritual immersion, they will be like the Marranos who converted from their own ancient Judaism to the Galician Judaism of

Agudat Yisrael and the Oriental Judaism of Shas, denying their own heritage.

The protesting Ethiopians held massive demonstrations opposite the august portals of the Chief Rabbinate in Jerusalem. In the courtyard fronting the building, across the street from the demonstrating Ethiopians, I met a friend, a civilized man. He didn't understand what all the fuss was about—after all, the Chief Rabbinate is showing compassion; it wants them "only" to undergo ritual immersion in order to ensure "their Jewishness."

Thus history repeats itself, and it is this Chief Rabbinate in all its Orthodoxy that proves to us that we are just like all other nations.

After 29 days and nights, on the evening of Thursday, October 3, 1985, the demonstration ended. The leaders of the bewildered but defiant Ethiopians—Adisso, Tuvia, Moshe, Rachamim, and others—had in their hands copies of a series of letters exchanged between chief rabbis Avraham Shapiro and Mordechai Eliahu, and Prime Minister Shimon Peres.[40]

The drama remains however, because the Ethiopians represented a larger struggle taking place for the image of Jewish society in Israel and throughout the international Jewish community.

Recently, a large scientific conference was held to mark the ninety-ninth birthday of David Ben-Gurion. Among the speakers was Dr. Yosef Burg, leader of the NRP and a veteran politician who worked together with Ben-Gurion virtually from the beginning of Israeli sovereignty. This doyen of religious-Orthodox politicians observed that in many ways Ben-Gurion had followed the Karaite line of thought. He believed in the Bible and rejected all biblical literature written in the days of the dispersion. Political Zionism is, therefore, at least partially a denial of the Jewish Talmudic culture that emanated from the restrictive compulsion of the Diaspora. Reform Judaism, to a degree, and of course Karaite Judaism and Ethiopian Judaism, are linked to the written Law—the Bible—and do not recognize the Talmud as binding theology.

Suddenly, it became clear that it is possible to preserve Judaism—even religious Judaism—in its pure almost extremist form, without recourse to the Talmud, which the Orthodox rabbinate controls in Israel, like a monopolistic Episcopalian church and under supreme religious Talmudic authority.

Before even we—the seekers after a sane Zionism— understood this, the Orthodox rabbis had already grasped that they must begin a destructive battle against the anti-Talmudic religious Jewish culture that stood before them in the guise of Ethiopian Jewry.

The Jewish roots of the Ethiopians are lost in the mists of antiquity. Some claim that owing to connections between King Solomon's kingdom and Ethiopia the pagan Ethiopians converted en masse to Judaism. The children of Israel indeed ruled Ethiopia with an iron fist for more than three and half centuries.

The Christian dynasties of the Ethiopian empire were influenced by Judaism and showed an affection for the Hebrew language. It is enough to recall that the last emperor, Haile Selassie I, had among his many grand titles that of "Lion of Judah," and that when he was defeated by the Italians in 1936 he took refuge in Jerusalem.

Rabbinical Orthodoxy has long been interested in Ethiopian Jewry. As far back as the ninth century A.D., the Jewish Dane Eldad described the rituals of the Ethiopian Jews.

In our own time, former Sephardic Chief Rabbi Ovadia Yosef recognized the Judaism of the Ethiopians. His adversary and partner on the rabbinical throne, Rabbi Shlomo Goren, also recognized the Jewishness of the Ethiopians and visited the site of their protest on a recent Yom Kippur.

The current Chief Rabbis are not really being contradictory. Their restriction on recognition of the Ethiopians springs from a desire to emphasize the submission of the Ethiopian Jews to Talmudic rabbinical leadership. Rabbinical Orthodoxy is determined to instill Talmudic understanding into traditional Ethiopian Jewry, and even to absorb the Ethiopian Jews into Talmudic Orthodoxy. It refuses to recognize the *kesim,* the clerical leaders of the Ethiopians, who led their flock through famine-ravaged Africa, but who are not considered suitably kosher to serve in religious offices, as marriage officers, members of the rabbinical tribunal, or teachers of the halacha to their own people.

The Orthodox rabbinate is prepared to show humanitarianism. It will waive symbolic circumcision and will "suffice" with ritual immersion, as long as its exclusive and unquestioned halachic authority as sole rabbinical authority (*poskim*) is acknowledged by the Ethiopians.

This is not the authority inherited from the early Jewish roots, in the days of the First Temple. On the contrary, it is a destruction of those roots and the conversion of the Ethiopians into Talmudic Jews. Here are some examples: Like Reform Jews, the Ethiopians, except for their leaders, do not cover their heads—neither on weekdays, nor on holidays, nor even in the house of prayer. Like the Karaite Jews, the dietary laws of the Ethiopians do not follow a system of separation of foods and utensils for meat and milk. The Ethiopian Sabbath is virtually identical to the Karaite Sabbath. To teach the Ethiopians the Talmudic Sabbath laws would be to convert them.

There is only one way of describing this situation. It

is religious coercion of religious Jews in the name of a competitive religion. For example, the Ethiopian Jews are rigid monogamists. It is doubtful if they would acknowledge the rabbi's permission to take a second wife.

It is untrue that the absence of a Talmudic interpretation of the Torah has left a lacuna in the religious understanding of the Ethiopians. The Jews of Ethiopia are unquestionably a "people of the Book." Their religious literature has developed over generations. It includes *The Pupils' Book* (*Sefer Ha'Talmidim*) commentary and other extra-biblical stories written in the ancient Amharic dialect. To make the Ethiopian Jews submit to Talmudic Orthodoxy is to estrange them from their ancient heritage.

Ironically, the "symbolic" conversion pressed upon the Ethiopians by the Chief Rabbinate is regarded by the latter as invalid, much as Reform conversion is invalid in the light of Talmudic halacha. By Orthodox definition, conversion for a specific reason is invalid. In this light, Reform conversion is invalid as it is often performed when one of the partners in a prospective marriage is not Jewish. The conversion of an Ethiopian couple in order to prepare them for the Jewish wedding ceremony is identically invalid. The difference between the two instances is that the Reform conversion whisked away from the Jewish "Episcopalian Church" control of those souls and the souls of their children, while in the case of the Ethiopians, the conversion will put an entire community safely into the grip of the rabbinate.

The purpose of the Chief Rabbinate is indecently transparent.

Orthodox concession to the Ethiopians means yielding the religious monopoly, and recognition of their distinctive Jewishness is a tacit acknowledgment of religious pluralism in Judaism. This would force recognition of the legitimacy of Reform, Conservative, and Karaite Jews, who openly reject the Talmud. At the cost of the Ethiopian heritage, therefore, the rabbis are fighting for religious Talmudic Orthodox monopoly.

The issue of the Ethiopians teaches all too clearly that Rabbinical Orthodox exclusivity is not an expression of the rule of law but a challenge to it.

Adoption

Adoption is another sphere where Rabbinical Orthodoxy rules supreme. Article 5 of the Child Adoption Act of 1981 states: "There shall not be adoption except from the same religion as the person who is adopting."[41]

A byproduct of this injunction is that a child without any religious affiliation cannot be adopted by someone with a definite affiliation. This means that children like Ilana Stern, Rina Eitani, the Shalit children, and the sons of the Argentinian immigrants could not be adopted by Jewish, Moslem, or Christian families in Israel.

How does this apply to children of Reform Jewish parents, where the mother was converted according to Reform precepts? Since there has not yet been any legal precedent for such an instance, it is reasonable to assume that a child of this union cannot be adopted by "pure" (in Orthodox terms) Jewish parents.

The permutations of this legal injunction are endless.

Burial

On the sweeping slopes of Jerusalem's Mount Scopus is a British military cemetery where the fallen of General Allenby's battalions in World War I are interred. The long rows of crosses are interspersed with stars of David. Soldiers who fought as brothers-in-arms were buried as brothers-in-arms.

Not so with Israelis. For them, segregation continues after death. The shadow touches even the IDF, a fighting force with a well-merited reputation for togetherness. Each IDF soldier goes into battle knowing that his fellows care as much about him as about themselves. But in the military cemeteries each is buried according to religion and ethnic origin. Sadly, this segregation holds rigidly for the non-Jewish fighting men—the Druse with their incomparable record of service, the Moslem Bedouin, and the Circassians.

The precept also extends to Jews. In accordance with the decree of the Orthodox military rabbinate, the soldier son of a Jewish father and a Gentile mother is buried separately from his more kosher coreligionists.

Civilian burial is legislated. Article 13 of the Jewish Religious Services Act[42] empowers the Minister of Religious Affairs to regulate the licensing of companies for Jewish funeral services. This provision, together with the Religious Communities Ordinance of 1926 (a British Mandate heritage), ensures that religion is the sole criterion for burial in Israel.

The special law dealing specifically with Jewish funeral companies was initiated by the NRP in 1966. Only the Minister of Religious Affairs can authorize establishment of funeral companies. Land for cemeteries is authorized by regional planning councils and distrubuted by the Israel Lands Authority, which owns more than 90 percent of the land in Israel. But sanction from both bodies is subject to the recommendation of the Ministry of Religious Affairs.

The practical result is that cemeteries and funeral services adhere rigidly to the tenets of religious Orthodoxy. A tacit agreement frees kibbutz private cemeteries of direct control, but the effect is minimal, as only 3.5 percent of the population is involved. This is the hard reality with which the Anghelevici family collided, and which shook Israeli public opinion.

The father of the Anghelevici family is a Jew; his Gentile wife was Christian Greek Orthodox. The devoted couple survived the Holocaust and came to Israel where they brought up their three children as Jews. One daughter died young and was buried in Rishon LeZion in a Jewish cemetery, her mixed origin apparently having escaped the eagle eye of the local rabbinate.

The mother had long identified with her husband's people, and asked her family to ensure that she be buried not in a Greek Orthodox cemetery but alongside her daughter. Upon her death she was duly buried in the Rishon LeZion Jewish cemetery. When the local rabbinate discovered her Gentile origin, they demanded that her body be exhumed. The surviving daughter fought to respect her late mother's wish, and succeeded in obtaining a Supreme Court order of injunction against the rabbinate's decision.

Attempting to compromise, the rabbinate suggested that the mother's body be reinterred just outside the cemetery, or even inside, although in a clearly separate plot. The family refused. In an atmosphere thick with threat and anger, the body was found one morning flung on the outskirts of a nearby Moslem cemetery.

The ghoulish criminals were discovered, tried, and convicted. The attorney general successfully appealed their light sentence. Support for the criminals grew, and a demonstration staged in front of the Tel Aviv District Court became violent to the point of contempt of court. Voiced repeatedly was the main argument that the secular state was attacking the sanctity of laws of the Torah, which had motivated the grave robbers.

The issue reached national proportions. Right-wing

groups supported the demand of the Orthodox camp that the felons be pardoned, arguing that they had acted in God's name. Eventually President Herzog intervened and granted the amnesty.

Public figures in Israel, identified as "secular," supported the Anghelevici family. They were joined by Reform rabbis Tuvia Ben-Horin and Moshe Zemer, but there was no organized protest from the non-Orthodox religious camp, despite the Reform movements having taken a formal stand on precisely this type of issue as long ago as 1918.

Unfortunately, as frequently happens in Israel when a highly emotional issue is at stake, public attention became diverted from the main problem to a peripheral one.

If the cemeteries were owned by the religious communities and synagogue-goers, it is doubtful whether the Anghelevici family would have had any claim, even on moral grounds. But this is not the case in Israel.

The law does not permit the establishment of cemeteries for nonreligious people, or people not wanting to be labeled with a formal religious identity before death. The burial of Jews was put in the hands of Orthodox monopolies, which gave precedence to the ethnic origin of the deceased rather than to personal attitudes. When the time comes for burial, there is no choice. A religious service is always required, and if a Jew is involved, it will be an Orthodox service.

Regardless of the wishes of the mother, or their own, the Anghelevici family had no choice because the law itself gave them no choice.

— 5 —
Back to the Ghetto

In his memoirs, Raymond Aron attempts to distinguish between two concepts: religious belief, and the dogmatism of "secular theologies" such as Marxism-Leninism and National Socialism. Whereas the former is not pinned under the blade of logic and we are not asked to treat it as material reality, the latter is gift-wrapped as material reality and the sciences. I am not convinced that Aron is correct in his distinction.

The Orthodox Jewish halachic understanding was aimed at afflicting the entire Jewish nation with 613 Commandments. Through the Torah and the Oral Law, the halacha presents the sole source of answers to all questions, whether in metaphysics, human behavior, or the sciences. Halacha is a "living doctrine," which without any limitations deems itself timeless. It determines the time of the world's creation and the origin of every living creature. It is not merely a manual guiding the daily life of the Orthodox Jew, but an exclusive outlook on life from which one draws all aspirations, all knowledge, and the answers to all questions. The halacha of the chief Orthodox rabbinical schools and the Council of Torah Sages has a "geology" of its own as well as its own "solutions" to scientific questions; they refuse even to consider theories such as those attributed to Darwin, Freud, and Einstein. No scientific discovery—geological, archaeological, astronomical, or biological—can even come close to contending with what is written in the Torah, which they believe to be a book of divine origin and, therefore, far superior to what the human mind is capable of inventing.

Although the humanistic world adopted these theories with the enthusiasm it shows to all inventions, discoveries, and new approaches to gaining knowledge, this goes hand in hand with the permanent need to question and the acceptance of doubt as a part of the living reality.[1]

The creationist halacha, the monumental Jewish-religious codification of rabbinical decisions through the ages, either has already given an answer to your question or is prepared to do so, by relying on rabbinical authorities interpreting the Torah and by rejecting any concept that contradicts previously established dogmatic principles. Halacha, in ruling on Orthodox interpretations, has no place either for stimulation regarding secular matters or for doubt, at least as far as *Deorayta,* the Divine Commandments, are concerned.

As long as this approach remains solely within the realm of believers, no problem arises. However, when their leaders desire to infuse their beliefs into the secular legal system by taking advantage of the most basic principles of democracy, then those who support humanism must make themselves heard.

When this type of understanding invades the mind of a nation, when it determines the order of intellectual preference by replacing arts and sciences with theology it becomes the kind of "ism" that has brought and will bring disaster on the people enslaved by it.

Mystical and dogmatic approaches claim a monopoly over our minds and our national lives. Although Jews are "commanded" in halacha not to be like the Gentiles, mind-controlling commandments like these, when allowed to develop as a political power among other civilizations in the past, have caused inconceivable disaster and trouble for many successive generations.

Some might claim it an injustice if the lofty human values, also incorporated in Orthodox Jewish halacha, are not commemorated. I feel, however, that there is no need to emphasize what is already common knowledge; it is of greater importance to deal with the damages and dangers of enforcing a narrow and binding lifestyle on an entire state and its citizens who are unwilling to accept it.

Mrs. Daniella Velancy, a woman loyal to her religious-Orthodox views and way of life, was a "prisoner of the rabbinic family-courts" in the State of Israel, struggling against the establishment that prevents her from receiving a rabbinic divorce from her husband. She is self-assured of her power to influence the Chief Rabbinate and the rabbinic courts "from within." So here, from within the Orthodox camp itself, come the voices of the moderates, liberals, and humanitarians protesting the vulgar attempt to instill divine belief in state law.

Professor Elyse Shalvy, principal of a public religious (Orthodox) high school in Jerusalem, and herself Orthodox, complains of the rigidity of the Chief Rabbinate, which avoids meeting the realistic challenges presented by claims of women's rights and tolerance. She did wonders in defining the rabbinate's approach as one of disregard, of playing the part of "the average man." From a personal point of view, it is a tragicomedy to learn of the deep inner discomfort of certain Orthodox Jews. Yet despite the presence of such personalities as Professor Shalvy and Mrs. Velancy in the religious-Orthodox sector, it must be emphasized that these people do not compose the task forces of the militant Orthodox, nor are they the ones who will halt the progession of the giant steamroller that crushes everything in its path. The two warring forces—the Orthodox and the secular camps—activate much stronger powers in the arena. Politics, economics, law, and governmental authority are drawn into the picture, with the Orthodox now having the upper hand. They are better united and more certain of their strength, and they enjoy privileges that the secularists consciously deny themselves.

Unfortunately, however, the anger of individuals cannot even hope to influence the rabbinic establishment. With regard to social phenomena, anger has no practical significance.

Having been born into the so-called "weaker sex," Velancy and Shalvy are a priori disqualified by Jewish religious Orthodoxy from heading a congregation and equally participating with men in a religious executive body. Moreover, both of these women and others like them sincerely believe, albeit mistakenly, that the actual dispute is over priorities and that the common moral denominator of the entire Jewish world has not been lost. Their error, in my opinion, stems from the very root of their assumption. They are still looking forward to rabbinic Orthodox "flexibility"—humanitarian solutions in specific cases—while the rabbinical courts are exercising measures considered by those dissidents as contradicting "modern needs." The dispute is no longer over individual humanitarian relief.

The alternative option is a humanistic value system based on the equality of all human beings and a constitutional polycentric principle of sovereignty of the people. This cannot be achieved under rabbinic authority. The dispute is an encounter between two forces, each of which claims to have total control over its camp. This is a "Kulturkampf"—a fact that cannot be disguised. The rift in the nation is a fact and will widen even more in the next generation. It is being forced on even the most sacred aspects of life: education, family, tradition, and culture.

This cultural confrontation continues to grow. The coalition agreements and the generosity of the Zionist regime have practically dropped power in the lap of the Orthodox camp. The moment this power was exercised, the secular constitutional establishment exhibited shock.

Teddy Kollek, mayor of Jerusalem, does not conceal his surprise. Whether real or fabricated, the naiveté with which he claims that "everything was fine" two years ago and that the religious attack occurred "suddenly" is not the issue. Action speaks louder than words, and the Orthodox actions we have witnessed did not begin this morning. There was no surprise attack on the part of the Orthodox, but rather deliberate blindness on our part to the slow, steady process of conquest. The Orthodox establishment did nothing to conceal its goals; it was the secular camp that exhibited weakness and helplessness and preferred to bury its head in the sand.

It is true that the religious public, under the extremist leadership of its rabbis and representatives throughout the regime, moved from gaining strength to exerting it. One needs no military or political training to reach such conclusions. The movement gained strength before our eyes and with the help of our own hands.

We are now witnessing the Judgment Day of the State's domestic affairs. While nobody is able to predict the future, the deviation from basic Zionist expectations looks evident.

Some Orthodox, mainly anti-Zionist, factions felt the Zionist movement, under socialist leadership, abused religious needs.

While shtetl-like behavior was considered unacceptable in the new-born Israel, religious-Orthodox rituals were sometimes identified with this Jewish way of life, which was felt not to meet the needs of the State of Israel as symbolized by "a new Jew"—the farmer, the soldier, the worker.

From this primary stage of inferiority, sometimes real and sometimes imaginary, the Orthodox reached a stage of gaining strength. They emerged as a powerful political factor monopolizing essential communal services and successfully channeling public funds to Orthodox institutions by legal means. At this point, the Orthodox religious camps graduated to the stage of an actual offensive. The more they recognized their power the more their extremism grew.

Mutually antagonistic Orthodox associations, groups, and factions with no common denominator have sprung up around us. The Neturei Karta, a small and ancient militant anti-Zionist Orthodox community of Jerusalem, and the Szatmar rabbi's ex-Hungarian rabbinical court are fiercely confronting the ultra-Orthodox Agudat Yisrael for accepting "Zionist money" and for actively participating in the Israeli political process. The Zionist Orthodox religious are encountering the non-Zionist Orthodoxy and suffering from Sephardi Torah Guardians on ballots as well as in day-by-day confrontations, while themselves launching successful campaigns against the status quo ante by introducing coercive laws against the non-Orthodox silent majority. The Orthodoxy is engaged in domestic quarrels even within the same creed, while each segment rejects some rituals and even ritual dietary food of its Orthodox opponent.

On certain issues, however, most Orthodox groups find themselves in the same camp. While the issue of "who is a Jew" emerges, while a Jewish Reform house of prayer is delivering a sermon under threat of violence, while a conservative community is waiting for a permit to build a synagogue in Jerusalem, while evolutionists confront creationists, while the Mormons build in Jerusalem an extension to Brigham Young University, and while the fundamentalist Sabbath is on the agenda, almost all of Orthodoxy joins the same team.

While the Orthodoxy affects the fragile political stability, the "socialists" strengthen the Orthodox troops by giving them secular legitimacy for a right Sabbath. Opportunistic political balance of power has priority over humanistic values. Thus, fulfillment of Zionist goals gave way to the demands of the violent religious fundamentalist groups.

It all began with political pressure, which gave rise to the assumption that it is possible to advance and face greater challenges. The doors were opened for the development of the ultra-Orthodox violence in Jerusalem and Bnei Brak and for religious-Orthodox pressure in general.

The leaders of Agudat Yisrael supported this violence and were active in exercising the pressure. Rabbi Eliezer Schach, spiritual leader of the Lithuanian sector of the ultra-Orthodox sect and of the Sephardic Shas party (an ultra-Orthodox Sephardi political faction), did a great deed when he told his God-fearing public: "Now is not the time for feelings. Awake, arise. Do not rest, and be not silent until the land is free from insolence and religious persecution."

The heads of the Gush Emunim movement for greater Israel, the National Religious Party (NRP), rabbis Waldman, Levinger, and Neriah, and their young followers consolidated with the protesters in favor of the purification of Temple Mount from solely Moslem presence and the construction of a synagogue there, even before the Jewish terror gang trial had been wiped from national memory.

The NRP-affiliated Chief Rabbi of Petach Tikva, who is a public servant appointed by a public-statutory body and paid by the government, leads a struggle paved with rallies against the operation of cinemas on the Sabbath and confronts police by inciting to illegal demonstrations.

If it is sufficient for wide circles of society to define the rule of law as a burden in order to depress elected institutes and stun the secular judicial authority, how much harsher can the truth be when one realizes that democracy is not a Jewish value, and when one sees the concept of understanding advancing toward violence based on theology?

The religious-Orthodox camp has a complete conception according to which the people of Israel and the Torah of Israel are inseparable. "Torah" is viewed as that which has been preserved in halachic literature. This approach developed a vocabulary that has played a major role in crystalizing the Orthodox consciousness. For example, according to the halachic definition, secularism is likened to death, as it is stated: "To separate between holy and secular" (Leviticus 10:10). Secularity is disgraced as an antithesis to holiness, an expression of vulgarity. A discussion of secular matters is tasteless, worthless. The relationship between a Talmudic Jew and a secular Jew is considered similar to relations between a Roman aristocrat and a barbarian. Hence anyone who isn't a Roman can only be a barbarian.

The non-Orthodox erroneously fell into the trap set for them by the religious establishment and adopted the term *secular* to describe themselves. From here, the way to creating a "popular" Orthodox consensus of avoidance and contempt for humanistic approaches was short.

The slide into uniformism created a deceptive terminology.

Many have naively believed until now that the savage world pictured by George Orwell[2] is in no way connected to the State of Israel. They think that only in the imagined totalitarian world of "Big Brother" does black mean white, love mean hate, and peace mean war. But in an atmosphere of cultural rift, each of the opponents condemns the other for corrupting the language. For example, the term *Israel* was always considered to mean the Jewish people, in expressions like "sons of Israel," "the destiny of Israel," and "the Israelite." But the modern polycentric-Zionist State of Israel usurped this meaningful word for secular needs. A citizen of the State of Israel bears an Israeli passport, holds Israeli citizenship, and properly is considered as an Israeli even if a Gentile (approximately 18 percent of the total population of the State of Israel is Gentile). The term *Hebrew*, historically synonymous with *Jew* and *Israelite*, was disconnected from this ethnocentric (religious-Orthodox) context. It describes the (modern) Hebrew language, the Hebrew Army (Ben-Gurion's expression), as well as Hebrew (Reform) congregations in America. The Orthodoxy lost a monopoly on this expression as well.

On the other hand, an Orthodox vocabulary, or an Orthodox-tailored one, has emerged. It includes terms such as the following:

Anti-Semite: one who desires to attend soccer games on the Sabbath at the national stadium in Ramat Gan; one who supports the building of a soccer stadium in Jerusalem; one who attempts to drive on the Sabbath; a patient hospitalized in Sha'arey Zedek Hospital who quietly expresses his desire to telephone his family on the Sabbath; anyone who supports the switch to Daylight Saving Time in the summer months.

Being a "Real" Jew: accepting halachic rulings.

Christian neophyte: a Jew who prays according to the Reform ritual.

Democracy: a rule borrowed from the Greeks that does not express the values of Judaism. Anyone who wants democracy should move to America.

Despiser of Israel: one who questions the importance of the Chief Rabbinate.

Ethiopian Jew rallying in Jerusalem: a black communist, properly compelled, who has not absorbed the significance of a "Jewish State" (see definition), and who is incited by the Despisers of Israel, Hellenistic anti-Semites, and Christian neophytes (see definitions).

Fight against assimilation: segregation and disconnection from liberalism, socialism, and Reform and Conservative Judaism.

Hellenist: a nonreligious Jew, sometimes known as an "apostate to anger." Hellenism includes sports, theatrical plays, books, and works of art—especially when exhibited on the Sabbath.

Jewish Culture: that and only that which the Orthodox consider "Jewish culture"—in short "Castel," meaning half casbah, half shtetl.

Jewish education: Orthodox Jewish education.

Jewish State: a Jewish Orthodox community under God within the borders of the State of Israel.

Love of Israel: Do not love thy neighbor unless he, like yourself, is an Orthodox Jew, or at least, as a Jew, constitutes a potential object for Orthodox missionary action.

Patience: the measure of constraint the religious public offers, in the meantime, toward refugees still under the influence of the Declaration of Independence on civilian life in Israel.

Sovereignty: Rabbinic rule.

Status quo: a springboard for the expansion of religious

influence in the State.

Tolerance: the display of tolerance for Orthodox intolerance.

Professor Shaul Ettinger, a noted Jerusalem historian who is studying the contemporary process of the survival of the Jewish people, is not at all surprised by the strength of efforts in education and the media that have been put to use in this great struggle.

He claims that Orthodox Judaism desires all of the credit for existing Jewish culture; however, if the Orthodox establishment were victorious, the Jewish people would shrink to 10 percent of its present size. Ninety percent of the Jewish people survived without being Orthodox—the free Zionists, the Reform and Conservative Jews, "the searchers," and those whose Judaism is dictated by the anti-Semites.

It was Orthodoxy that did not allow adaptation to changing realities. It became fossilized in the same way that Karaite Judaism became petrified in its time. The healthy instinct of survival that led the Jewish people for centuries commanded separation from Orthodoxy. Thus, the Jews were saved as a nation. The question we must answer in Israel today is whether we have learned the lessons history has taught us, or if there is evidence in modern Israel of a self-destructive process. Have we agreed to be sucked into the Orthodox whirlpool in order to drown with it? The way to the bottom of this whirlpool, if we so choose, will be paved with confrontation in the international sphere as well.

The Orthodox ghetto promotes self-imposed xenophobia and alienation from European humanistic tradition from philosophies that encourage scientific curiosity and appreciation of the arts. The Orthodox "Episcopal Jewish Church" has stamped these phenomena with the shameful seal of Hellenization. The result is the widening rift between Israel and the

Western world, not to mention the split between the Orthodox Jews of Israel and the non-Orthodox Jews in the Diaspora.

When the noted Israeli poet Nathan Alterman spoke with Zionist leaders about "normalization" of the Jewish People, he meant more than just rejecting exile. Some people even accused the midstream of Zionism, and Ben-Gurion of Canaanism, by disconnecting from the Diaspora Jews.

Today, while Israel goes through a process of "ghetto-ization," and the great spread throughout the United States and Canada becomes the stronghold of Jewish pluralism, isolation will be the symbol of the Orthodox cult and its Messianic outshoots within Israel. The events of the thirty-first Zionist Congress stand as living proof. Reform and Conservative factions joined with the Zionist Labor party and succeeded in passing a declarative decision on the right of Jewish religious pluralism. In effect, although no more than a repetition of what was stated in Israel's Declaration of Independence, the decision was a challenge to the monopoly of contemporary Jewish spiritual life.

The practical result followed shortly: Those same "lovers of Israel," who had always claimed the joint security and extraterritorial common fate of all Jews wherever they might be, gathered together against "American" interference in Jewish life and demanded the "Israelization" of the Zionist movement.

Paradoxically, the awakening of the Reform Movement in the United States and the new spirit of this movement in Israel could be setting a new trend. They could, however, represent only a temporary phase that will pass with the coming of a new day.

Milovan Djilas, the communist who accompanied Joseph Broz Tito until they parted with the slam of a door, criticized modern communism. In his book, *The New Class,* he wrote:

The assumption that Marxism is a universal trend—
an assumption that the Communists cling to—can
only cause tyranny in all spheres of intellectual activity.
What will the luckless physicists do if the atoms do
not behave in accordance with the Marxist-Hegel
Theory or with the theory of "opposites attract and
develop into more sophisticated forms"?

What will they do . . . if the Cosmos remains
indifferent to Communist dialects?

And what of the biologists, if the flora does not
behave according to the Stalinistic Theory of Lysenko
. . . and if these people of science are unable to lie
. . . why, they will have to suffer the consequences
of their "heresy." . . . The people of science are faced
with a never-ending dilemma lest their ideas and
discoveries harm one of the principles of the official
theory. Therefore, they are trapped against their will,
into compromising their scientific ideas. . . . In many
ways, modern Communism resembles the seclusion
of religious schools in the Middle Ages.[3]

George Orwell (pen name of the British author Eric Blair)
preceded Djilas in expounding on the totalitarianism that
would suffocate man's existence and freedom of choice, of
doubt, of creation.

His book *1984* is a forecast of the totalitarian regime's
conquest over our private lives by virtue of the world-
encompassing ideology: that which presents the plain and
simple truth. Penetration into private lives is carried out
through the mechanisms of modern technology, to ensure
loyalty to "Big Brother" and to enable the people to "repent"
in time to be acceptable according to the directives of the
ideological designers in control.

Professor Jacob Talmon, father of "Totalitarian Democracy"[4] describes totalitarianism as "dictatorship carried on the

waves of public enthusiasm" and of "Messianic belief." This is the reign of idealistic dictatorship. Let us not be led to believe that this is a modern invention. Rather, this hideous modern philosophy grew out of the Inquisition, which nurtured theological brainwashing and claimed the high price of enslaving the spirit and spilling innocent blood.

Talmon differentiates between totalitarianism of the political Right and the Left. He believes that the latter, in principle, was always "and still is today, concentrated on man, human logic and human salvation. . . ." Right totalitarianism dealt with "the communal unit, the State, the nationality and the creed."

Talmon claims that totalitarianism of the Right is needed only by historical, racial, or organizational units. The divine, mystical, metaphysical identity between the Jewish religion and nationality, which is nourished directly from the history of a chosen people, exists to build, under recognized political circumstances, a totalitarian approach. Talmon believes that the Left always inclines toward a universal view, whereas the Right, in its totalitarian guise, opposes universalism. The latter stands for pragmatism, which permits an ethnic, religious, or nationalist group to exist to its fullest potential while ignoring other external groups. Right totalitarianism sees man as a weak and corrupt creature: "One must use strength as a constant means of preserving order among those destitute creatures who are given to fighting and contentions in order to prepare them to rise above their natural weakness." Talmon concludes with a pronounced fear that religious Messianism bears within it seeds of totalitarianism.

Totalitarianism cannot exist without conceptual zeal and brutal violence. These herd the nation into complete totalitarianism by uniting divisions and by opposing various social institutions and powers using totalitarian ideology, allowing for traditional validation of savagery and the annihilation of deviant thought.

Yosef Shamir[5] deems totalitarianism as the curse of our century. Totalitarianism, under whatever name it chooses, contains the foundation of surrender, subjection, and enslavement. Religious totalitarianism has an added factor since it envisions itself obligated by virtue of its divine origin to imprison the human spirit so that it should not deviate from "the right path."

However, despite the erosion of cultural structure caused by the Inquisition, despite the Holocaust that sprang from the Nazi regime, despite the work camps and mental hospitals for opposers of the regime in the Soviet Union, we are witnesses to the religious Islamic totalitarian victory in Iran and to the strengthening of fundamentalist-religious principles in Egypt.

At times it appears that people desire to be controlled and that they dread freedom of thought, preferring in its stead the warm, secure blanket of the ruler who will tell them what to do, how to think, and in what to believe, and who will solve any problems once and for all.

Notwithstanding the differences among them, totalitarian approaches repel humanism by viewing the human being as a weak, spineless creature who must be coercively educated, directed, and guided to open the doors of true redemption to him.

These philosophies do not come out of thin air. Western European Marxism went through a period of "adjustment" in Soviet Russia, in part due to the roots that sprang from czarist despotism and Byzantine culture.

One must consider what will become of an Israeli democracy that lacks a Bill of Rights and as a result of its Talmudic and ghetto roots that dictate segregation, xenophobia, a sense of uniqueness, and repel the principles of equality that the political institution is so eager to adopt as a recommended social norm.

Haim Peles, an Israeli Orthodox religious thinker, sees Israel's isolation as an act of divine grace. He writes: "The people of Israel are presently in such a state that a formal peace with the Arabs will bring about assimilation . . . in the Semitic region. Consequently, we may see in the state of war between us and the Arabs the hand of Providence."[6] The road to Messianism as a substitute for revelation and to elevation as a substitute for control is not long.

Yehoshafat Harkabi says that the "pretense" that historic process begins only with others and that the people of Israel are not subject to this process and are free from historic "law" is only one step away from receiving unrealism as a principle.[7]

Rubinstein, a liberal politician and a scholar, follows Harkabi's pessimism by revisiting the Zionist dream, concluding that Zionism means: "a home and not a temple, a secular nation and not a sacred tribe, a good neighbor . . . and not a recluse destined and willing to reside alone." He continues: "Israel will be measured and its future will depend on its will and ability to return to these old truths."[8] But is Israeli society really able and willing to proceed to reach this goal?

Epilogue

Rabbi Morton Berman, a noted Reform rabbi and leading Zionist from the United States who settled in Israel several years ago, died in January 1986 and was buried in the cemetery on the Mount of Olives in Jerusalem.

On the morning of Tuesday, February 25, prior to the afternoon service for the consecration of the headstone, members of Rabbi Berman's family visited his gravesite. They found the grave surrounded by a cement wall.

The wall was erected on instructions from ultra-Orthodox haredi leaders. During the previous few days posters had been displayed through Jerusalem's Mea Shearim quarter, objecting to Rabbi Berman's burial in the Mount of Olives cemetery and ordering the wall built "to separate the unclean grave" from the others.[1]

Notes

Abbreviations Used in the Notes

BT: *Babylonian Talmud.*
ET: *Encylopedia Talmudica.*
ILB: *Israeli Law Book (Sefer Ha'Hukim).*
ILR: *Law Reports* of the Israeli Supreme Court *(Piskey Din).*
RKP: *Records* of Knesset Proceedings *(Divrey Ha'Knesset).*

Introduction

1. It is beyond any doubt that the halachic-Talmudic reasoning is reached by considering a variety of opinions, hence the sophisticated rabbinical "responsa" —questions and answers—are regarded as the very essence of halachic Judaism. But by the same token, this Judaism cruelly rejects, prohibits, and excommunicates any step or expression that collides with the legalistic-dogmatic concept of Orthodox Judaism, which is xenophobic and intolerant by definition, as expressed by the Orthodox rabbinical establishment.

2. Raphaela Bilski-Ben Hur, *Every Individual is a King: The Social and Political Thought of Zeev (Vladimir) Jabotinsky* (Tel Aviv: Dvir Publishing House, 1988) (Hebrew).

3. David Singer, "American Jews as Voters: The 1986 Elections," notes that social class and religiosity all played roles in how different groups of Jews voted (*Stark Jewish News*, February 1987), p. 13.

Chapter One: Escape from the Ghetto

1. Jacob Katz, *Out of the Ghetto: Background for Jewish Emancipation, 1770–1870* (Tel Aviv: Am-Oved Publishing House, 1985) (Hebrew).
2. Rabbi David Polish, *Renew Our Days: The Zionist Issue in Reform Judaism* (Jerusalem: World Zionist Organization in Cooperation with the World Union for Progressive Judaism, 1976).

Chapter Two: From State Sovereignty to Rabbinical Entity

1. Eliezer Schweid, *Democracy and Halacha: A Study in the Thought of Rabbi Haim Hirschensohn* (Jerusalem: Magnes Press, 1978) (Hebrew). Eliezer Schweid, *Judaism and Secular Culture* (Tel Aviv: Hakibbutz Hameuchad Publishing House Ltd., 1981) (Hebrew). Ze'ev Falk, *Dat HaNetzach v'Tzarchei Ha-Sha'ah/The Eternal Religion and Contemporary Needs* (Jerusalem: Mishrin Publications, 5746) (Hebrew).
2. Schweid, *Hirschensohn*, p. 84.
3. *Tractate Sanhedrin*, p. 26, col. A of *Babylonian Talmud* (Jerusalem: Yad Harav Hertzog Publishing House, 5745) (hereafter cited as *BT*).
4. Rabbinical Judges Act 5715–1955, *Israeli Law Book*, 179: p. 135, (hereafter cited as *ILB*).
5. Rabbi Arieh HaLevi Herzog, "Restrictions in the Laws of Sovereign," *Torah U 'Medinah/Torah and State* 7–8 (Jerusalem: Chief Rabbinate, 5715–6), p. 9.
6. Records of *Knesset Proceedings*, col. 41, p. 341 (session of November 16, 1964) (hereafter cited as *RKP*).
7. Law concerning Matzoh Feast (restriction on leaven) 5746–1986, *ILB*, 1191, p. 220. Two members of Knesset who initiated this legislation, Prof. Avner Hay Shaki (NRP) and Abraham Shapiro (Agudat Yisrael), explained the necessity of this proposal by saying that the display of leavened products during Passover hurts the "religious, traditional and national feelings." *Hatzaot Hok/Bills,* 1724, p. 160, April 4, 1985 hereafter cited as *Bills*).

8. On the halachic principle, "Dina d'malkhuta dina" ("The law of the ruler is binding") in: *Tractate Nedarim*, p. 28, col. A of *BT*; *Tractate Gittin*, p. 10, col. B of *BT*. See also: Shmuel Shiloh, *Dina d'malkhuta dina* (Jerusalem: The Academic Press, 1974). Shmuel Weingarten, "The Laws of the State and Their Validity According to Halacha," *Torah U'Medinah*, 5–6 (Jerusalem: Chief Rabbinate, 5713–4), pp. 306–30. Nathan Rath, "The Legal Status and Powers of Elected Representatives in Public Institutions and Bodies in Light of Halacha," *Shvilin* 16, 29–31 (Tel Aviv: Union of Rabbis in Israel, 5737), p. 110. Yitzhak Menahem Ginzburg, *Mishpatim B'Yisrael/Jewish Law* (Jerusalem: Harry Fishel Institute, 5716), pp. 66–70. Rabbi Ezra Batzri, *Dinei Mamonoth/Monetary Laws*, vol. 1 (Jerusalem: R. Mass Publications, 5734), p. 346, in which the author points to the civil legal system of the State of Israel and expresses his opinion that this is a Gentile instance.

Rabbi Ovadia Yossef, *Yichveh Da'at, Sh'aylot U'teshuvot/Responsa*, part D (Jerusalem: private publication), pp. 308–14, par. 65, states, "Therefore it is utterly forbidden to be judged by all these laws before an instance which judges according to Gentile law, which is ignorant, and there is no difference whether the judges are Gentiles or Jews who judge according to Gentile law which is not the Law of Torah." Indeed, justification is found in the Law of the State of Israel under the category of "regulation," or subsidiary legislation. This is expressed in halachic articles including: Chief Rabbi Avraham Shapira, "A Toraic Look at the Laws of the State and the Making of Regulations Today," *Tehumin*, vol. 3 (Alon Shevut, Gush Etzion: Zomet Publications, 5742), p. 238.

See also: *HaZofeh* of 17 April 1983. Moshe Silberg, "Law in the Hebrew State," *Ha'Aretz* of 17 February 1938 and 13 April 1938, and in his book *B'Ain K'Echad* (Jerusalem: Magnes Press, 5742), pp. 180–201. Gershon Weiler, *Teocratia Yehudit/Jewish Theocracy* (Tel Aviv: Am-Oved Publishing House, Ofakkim Series, 1977), pp. 163–79. Yitzhak Englard, "Incorporation of the Jewish Law in the Israeli Judicial System," in *B'Hagut U'V'Halacha/In Thought and in Halacha* (Jerusalem: Jewish Agency, Department for Toraic Culture, Ministry of Education, 5728), p. 168 and n. 4. Yitzhak Olshan, *Din U'Devarim/Dispute* (Tel Aviv: Shocken Press, 5738), pp. 169–71 and response by Moshe Una (then member of Knesset) *HaZofeh* of 30 November 1978. Yedidyah Cohen, *Dinei Yisrael/The Laws of Israel* (A yearbook for Jewish Law and for Family Law), vol. 6 (Tel Aviv: Tel Aviv University, 5735–1975), p. 127. Moshe Shawah, "Is a Deviation from or an Ignoring of the Secular Law's Provision, Which is Specifically Directed to the Rabbinic Court by the Secular Legislator, creating an 'Ultra-vires' Situation?" *HaPraklit* 28, 3 (Tel Aviv: Bar Association, 1973), pp. 299–316. Rabbi Haim David HaLevy, *Dvar HaMishpat/On Jurisprudence*, part 3 (Tel Aviv: private publication, n.d.), pp. 176–81. Eliyahu Cesare Ben-Zimra, "On Parliament and Constitution in Halachic Law," *Deoth/Opinions* 39 (5724), pp. 254–56 (A religious academic periodical). Menachem Eilon,

HaMishpat HaIvri/Hebrew Law, vol. 1 (Jerusalem: Magnes Press, 5733), pp. 120–21.

9. Adam Doron, "Democracy and Religious Legislation," *Avnaim* (Kfar Saba: Beit Berl, Spring 5726–1966), pp. 90–96. Amnon Rubinstein, "Law and Religion in Israel," *Israel Law Review* 2, no. 3 (July 1967), p. 381.

10. Act concerning restriction of pig raising 5722-1962 in *ILB* 377, p. 106. The reference here is to MK Yitzhak Artzi of the Labor Party Alignment (later the Center Party), a leader of the Independent Liberal Party. *Al HaMishmar* (hereafter cited as the *Daily Guardian*, weekend supplement of 16 December 1985).

11. *Yedioth Aharonoth*, 24 December 1985.

12. Rabbi Haim David HaLevy, *A'seh Lekha Rav/Appoint Yourself a Rabbi*, vol. 5 (Tel Aviv: Dvir Publications, 5727), pp. 32–43. Rabbi Haim David HaLevy, *A'seh Lekha Rav*, vol. 5, pp. 343–44 and 396. Rabbi Haim David HaLevy in *Mekkor Chayim HaShalem/The Complete Mekkor Chayim*, vol. 2, chap. 71, par. 14 (Tel Aviv: private publication, n.d.). Shlomo Aviner, *Am K'Lavi/Nation like a Lion*, vol. 1, par. 152 (Jerusalem: private publication, 5743–1983) pp. 126–29. Aviner, a prominent neo-Orthodox scholar, in his yeshiva advocates an "iron fist" against the Arab "hostile inhabitants" of Judea, Samaria, and Gaza. He supports his demands by theological-halachic reasoning based on Maimonides. Regarding his rabbinical opinion, one is not obliged to obey a law that contradicts the very essence of Judaism, see *Ha'Aretz*, 15 June 1984. Prof. Nahum Rakover, *Agency & Proxy in the Hebrew Law/Ha Shlihut Ve B'Mishpat HaIvri* (Jerusalem: Ha'Rav Kook Publishing House, 5752).

13. Based upon the biblical source *Leviticus* 5:21 and 25:17. *Tractate Baba Metzia*, p. 59, col. 1, of *BT*. For the definition of "colleague to Torah and Commandments," see *Tosefta Shavuoth*, chapter on Ritual Law 6, *Tractate Shavuoth*, p. 30, col. 1 of *BT*. Maimonides, *Hilkhot Evel/Laws of Mourning*, chap. 14, based on the same source in *BT*, i.e., *Tractate Pessachim*, p. 114, col. B. Maimonides, "Laws Regarding a Murderer and Preserving the Soul," chap. 13, law 14. Avraham Sherman, "The Relation of Halacha toward Our Brothers Who Abandoned the Path of Torah and Commandments," *Tehumin*, vol. A (Alon Shevut, Gush Etzion: Zomet Publications, 5740), pp. 311–13. Shalom Rosenberg,"You Went in His Way," in *Philosophia Yisraelit/Israeli Philosophy* (Tel Aviv: Papyrus Publications, 5743), p. 75, and especially note 12, p. 79. *Encyclopedia Talmudica* (a digest of halachic literature and Jewish law from early times to the present) (Jerusalem: Yad Harav Hertzog Publishing House, 1964–84), vol. A., *s.v.* "Ach" (brother), pp. 203–3. Hebrew and English editions; hererafter cited as *ET*.) On the problem of accepting the secularists as brothers in our time, see Menahem Rackman, "Mutual Appreciation and Unity," in *HaZofeh*, 7 September 1983.

14. Yeshayahu Leibowitz, *Al Emunah, Historia V'Arachim/On Faith, His-*

tory, and Values (Hebrew) (Jerusalem: Akkademon Press, 5742), pp. 181–86 and 187ff. On tolerance see also: Betty Roitman, "Against Tolerance," *Ma'ariv*, 23 July 1986. Nathan Rotenstreich, "Tolerance and Compromise," *Moznaim*, vol. 47, 3–4 (Tel Aviv: Authors' Society, Av-Elul, 5738), pp. 176–82 and "Tolerance and Beyond," *Ma'ariv* of 1 April 1983.

On halachic views of tolerance see also: Rabbi Dov Ber Soloveitchick, *Divrei Hagut V'Ha'aracha / Views and Assessments* (Jerusalem: Jewish Agency Department for Toraic Culture, 5742), p. 257. Eliezer Schweid, "Pluralism and Unification in Jewish Culture," *Moznaim*, 3–4 (Tel Aviv: Authors' Society, 1983), pp. 30–34. *Ad Mashber / Until Crisis* (Jerusalem: Jacques Publications, 1969), pp. 70–73. Alexander Altman, "Jewish Tolerance and Tradition within Judaism," *Panim Shel Yehadut / Faces of Judaism* (Tel Aviv: Am-Oved Publishing House, Ofakkim Series, 5743), pp. 217–32. Nathan Rotenstreich, *Yiumin B'Orchot HaZman V'HaChevra Ha Yisraelit / Reflections on Perspective and Israeli Society* (Tel Aviv: Am-Oved Publishing House, Ofakkim Series, 5730), p. 145. Amnon Rubinstein, "Is the Outlook for the Future a Positive One?" *Ha'Aretz* of 7 April 1982.

15. See also interview with the president of Israel, Haim Herzog, the *Daily Guardian* of 7 September 1983 and *Ha'Aretz* of 5 August 1983.

16. Moshe Kol, *Davar* of 17 March 1983. In the past Mr. Kol was the head of the famous "Youth Aliyah" network, and the Minister of Tourism and Development in various Israeli governments. He is one of the few signators of the Israeli Declaration of Independence who is still alive today. Chief Rabbi Mordekhai Eliyahu, "I Don't Squeal,"*Ha'Aretz* of 16 October 1985. Zerach Warhaftig, "Child-bride Marriages in Israeli Law in Comparison with Other Laws" (dissertation submitted to the Faculty of Law, Hebrew University, Jerusalem). Haim Ze'ev Reinas, "The Marriage of Minors as Found in the Talmud," *The Sapperstein Book* (Tel Aviv: Newman Press, 5730), pp. 191–200.

17. *Koteret Rashit / Headlines* of 30 October 1985, and *ET, s.v.* "Herem" (excommunication), vol. 17, p. 333. Menahem Ginzburg, *Mishpatim L'Yisrael*, pp. 66–70. See also "Hoshen Mishpat," commentary 26, part 1 in *Shulhan Arukh*: "It is forbidden to be tried before idolatrous judges and their instances, even if they are judging in accordance with Jewish traditional laws, and even if all the parties concerned accepted their jurisdiction, and any person who comes to be tried before it is evil and it is as if he reproached, abused, or lifted a hand to Moses' Torah." Kalman Cahana, "The Death Penalty and Its Implications," *Chekker V'Yiun / Research and Study*, vol. A (Jerusalem: private publication, 5720), p. 203. *ET*, vol. 3, *s.v.* "Beit Din" (rabbinic court), p. 156 and note 197. Benjamin Silber, *Az Nidbaru / They Were Spoken Of*, vol. 3 (Bnei Brak: private publication), p. 160. Rabbi Ovadia Yossef, *Rabbinic Responsa*, vol. 4 (Jerusalem: private publication, 5741), par. 65, pp. 306–14. Shulamit Har-Even, "Laws and Norms," *Yedioth Aharonoth* of 8 March 1985.

18. Then-Chief Rabbi Ben Zion Meir Hay Uziel: *Sha'arei Uziel / The Gates*

of Uziel (Jerusalem: HaRav Kook Publications) Vol. I: 1944; Vol. II: 1946; part 2, Introduction, p. 3.

19. Then-Chief Rabbi Shlomo Goren, "The Struggle over Hebrew in Hasmonean Times," *Ha'Aretz* of 8 December 1985. (Tel Aviv: Chief Military Rabbinate, 5727). Also, it is of utmost importance to note that Hanukah is an anti-West holiday. See Benjamin Zvielli, "Are We Not Hellenized?" in *HaZofeh* of 17 December 1982, on the trend to present the Hasmonean War as an antithesis to the miracle of Hanukkah. Shmuel Almog, *Zionut V'Historia/Zionism and History* (Jerusalem: Magnes Press, 5742), p. 23 and in general on the relationship of halacha to Gentile thought in the eyes of the Sages of Israel. Moshe Arens, *Reading Education* (Haifa: Haifa University, 5731), pamphlet 28, pp. 51–62. Dov Rapel, "Be Alert to Study the Law . . .What to Answer the Apostate— Metamorphosis of Educational Confusion," *Tehumin*, vol. C (Alon Shevut, Gush Etzion: Zomet Publications, 5742), pp. 477–84. Mordechai Broyer, "Prevent Your Children from Logic," in *The Stain of David—Memorial Issue for David Oakes* (Ramat Gan: Bar Ilan University, 5736), pp. 242–45. *ET*, vol. 19, *s.v.* "Chochmot Chitzoniyot" (external wisdom), pp. 55. Rabbi Shlomo Goren, "Judaism against Greek Philosophy," *Mahanayim*, pamphlet 112 (Tel Aviv: Military Rabbinate.)

20. Opposing the trend to attribute tragedies to Israel when it commits a transgression, see Yael Lotan, "Those Who Bow to Moloch," in the *Daily Guardian* of 28 June 1985.

21. *Kol Yerushalayim/ The Voice of Jerusalem* of 18 October 1985.

22. *Erev Shabbat* (weekly) of 18 October 1985.

23. Rabbi Richard Hirsch, "A Response to Rabbi Louis Bernstein," *Religion and Democracy*, Forum No. 44, p. 92.

24. Benjamin Zvielli, "The Wise Man Forgotten—Fifty Years after the Death of Rabbi Haim Hirschensohn," *HaZofeh* of 10 January 1986.

25. The Law of judgement of the Rabbinical Tribunals (Marriage and Divorce) 5713–1953, *ILB*, 134, p. 165.

26. The Jewish Religious Services Law (consolidated version) 5713–1971, in *ILB*, 628, p. 130.

27. High Court of Justice 516/75—Ben Horin and others v. Ministry of Religion. *ILB* 30 (2), p. 490.

28. Regarding the struggle in the Jerusalem neighborhood of Ramot over apportioning of land for a conservative synagogue, see articles in various local newspapers.

29. Rabbi Uri Regev (Dean of Hebrew Union College, Jerusalem), "Reform Marriage—Validity in Israel according to the Torah Law of Sanctifications and Marriages Held by a Rabbi Affiliated with the Movement for Progressive Judaism in Israel" (Jerusalem: Hebrew Union College, Institute for Judaic Studies, 5744), pp. 19–21.

30. The chair of the Parliamentary Commission on the state's Comptroller,

interpellations and answers. According to the Coalition Agreement of 1 August 1981 (par. 48), a total of 700 million shekels was to be channeled to the Orthodox religious educational institutions. As a response to two separate interpellations, the Treasury of the State of Israel furnished the Knesset with some details: in fiscal year 1981, 240 million shekels were transferred to the Orthodox religious institutions; in fiscal year 1982, 700 million shekels. *RKP*, p. 800, 3 January 1983, and p. 3219, 26 July 1983.

31. Teddy Kollek, *Kol Yerushalayim* of 27 December 1985.

32. Interview with Yigael Yadin, *Kol Yerushalayim* of 27 December 1985.

33. Rabbi Marvin Friedman, the *Jewish Press* (New York) 13 May 1983.

34. The *Jerusalem Post* of 6 May 1983.

35. Arnold Toynbee, *The World and the West* (New York/London: Oxford University Press, 1953), p. 26.

36. Aluf Har-Even, "Israeli Identification in the 21st Century," *Ha'Aretz* of 28 March 1983.

37. Rabbi Shlomo Goren in a series of articles, "The Archaeological Digs as Reflected in Truth and Halacha," *HaZofeh* of 29 July 1983. Article opposing Rabbi Goren's claims and methods in Ephraim Elimelech Auerbach's article, "For Zion Will Not Be Silent," *Ma'ariv* of 4 September 1981.

38. The *Jerusalem Post* of 6 May 1983.

39. The *Jerusalem Post* of 19 August 1983.

40. The *Jerusalem Post* local supplement of 19 August 1983.

41. Nurit Dovrat in *Ma'ariv* of 18 May 1986 describes the religious educators' fear of the study of foreign languages and exact sciences. See additional articles including that regarding the conflict between religious and secularists in education, *Ma'ariv* of 27 June 1986.

42. Uri Huppert, "Handel's Oratorio, and Sports: How They Affect the Trade Union," *BaMoatzah/In the Council* of 8 September 1983, issue 26.

43. Penal Law Amendment (Enticement to Change Religion) 5738–1977, *ILB,* 880, p. 50. The bill and the explanatory note were published in *Bills*, 1313, p. 40.

44. Regarding Chabbad (the Lubavitcher Rabbi's organization) as the initiator of the Return to Jewish Religion Movement, see Berke Wolf, spokesman for Chabbad, in a newspaper interview given to Ran Kislev in *Ha'Aretz* of 30 March 1984.

45. In an unprecedented act regarding relations with the State of Israel, 154 members of the U.S. Congress, including 18 members of the Congressional Committee on Foreign Affairs, 11 members of the Subcommittee for European Middle Eastern affairs, and 13 members of the Congressional Budget Committee, signed a petition on 8 May 1986 addressed to their Israeli colleagues, Knesset members, which opened as follows: "We have become increasingly concerned by reports here in the United States concerning certain groups in Israel who have undertaken a campaign to halt the construction and use of the Brigham

Young University Center for Near Eastern Studies currently under construction in Jerusalem. . . ."

46. Rabbi Shlomo Goren (then-Chief Chaplain of Israeli Defense Forces) in *Ha'Aretz* of 6 March 1956.

47. The *Jerusalem Post* of 13 August 1986.

48. "Religious Cossacks: is a literal translation of the Hebrew expression "Cossakim shel kadosh-baruch-Hu" used by non-Orthodox inhabitants of Jerusalem in addressing the ultra-Orthodox.

49. Law Prohibiting Fraud in Kashrut (Dietary Laws), 5753-1983, *ILB*, 1088, p. 128, 27 July 1983.

50. International Convention on the Elimination of All Forms of Racial Discrimination, 1966, ratified on 3 January 1979 by Israel.

51. *Genesis* 1:27.

52. *Leviticus* 19:18. *Tractate Pessahim*, p. 114, col. B, *BT*, and *Tractate Arakhim*, p. 16, col. B, of *BT*. Maimonides, *Laws of Knowledge*, chap. 6. Haim Pardess, "Hate Not Thy Brother," *HaZofeh* of 11 February 1983. Yisrael Newman, "Love of Israel above Hate of Israel," *Shanah B'Shanah/Year in Year Out*, vol. 25 (Jerusalem: Heichal Shlomo, 5744), p. 287–288. Shlomo Goren, "Love and Unfounded Hatred in Light of Halacha," *HaZofeh* of 30 July 1984. Ezra Batzri, *Responsa of the Gates of Ezra*, chap. 128, p. 416.

On the face of it, the International Convention on the Elimination of All Forms of Racial Discrimination fits the famous Rabbi Akiba's expression and fits the Talmudic humanistic expressions quoted in the explanatory notes to the bill against racial incitement, contributing very strongly to a common constitutional-humanistic denominator.

The words of *Genesis* (1:27) that "God created man in His own image, in the image of God," are considered as the foundation and source of the moral imperatives of the Holy Bible. If man is created in the image of God, then all men have the image of God and all are equal. Three important biblical sayings must be mentioned in this respect:

> "One law shall be to him that is homeborn, and unto the stranger that sojourned among you." (*Exodus,* 12:49)

> "Thou shalt not vex a stranger, nor oppress him, for ye were strangers in the land of Egypt. Ye shall not afflict any widow, or fatherless child." (*Exodus,* 22:20–21)

> "Thou shalt not oppress a hired servant that is poor and needy, whether he be of thy brethren or of thy strangers, that are in thy land within thy gates." (*Deuteronomy,* 24:14)

But these humanistic principles, as far as the halacha is concerned, are binding because of pragmatic needs of the Jewish community and not necessarily because of principles of equality, which are rejected. A Jew is "different" from a Gentile, a Jewish male is "different" from a woman (to be considered "sometimes as an unclean creature"), a Jew following God's Commandments is superior to an "apostate to anger," an average Jew, and a Jew considered as bastard are restricted in their relations, and so forth. A woman is "unclean" during her menstrual period, while dogs and pigs are perpetually unclean *(Shulhan Arukh*, "Laws of Clothing and Dress"). With regard to restrictions on saving the life of a Gentile woman, see Rabbi Moshe Isserles and Yoreh Deah (paragraph *kuf-nun-bet*). On the invalidity of a female to act as a witness, see Maimonides, "The Law of Witnessing" in *Yad Hazakah/Strong Hand*, chap. 9, Laws A and B. On restrictions on humanitarian first aid to Gentiles on the Sabbath, see "Way of Life and Ritual on the Sabbath," in *Mishnah Brurah*, paragraph 330: 1–2. Shaul Eisenstadt, "On the Question of Women's Rights," *HaIsha/The Woman*, issue 4–5 (Tammuz-Av, 5685), pp. 4–6ff, and comments on the Bill of Law for Equal Rights for Women, Memorandum to the Constitution, Law and Justice Committee of the Knesset, *Tziyun BaMishpat* (Tel Aviv, 5727), pp. 184–91. Reuven Katz, "Rights and Obligations of Husband and Wife," HaPardess, 25th anniversary edition (New York: 5714), pp. 349–52.

53. Rabbi Eric Yoffe, "Promoting Racism in Israel," *Shema* (monthly), New York 13/252, 15 April 1983.

54. *ET*, vol. 14, *s.v.* "Hovah" (obligation), pp. 228–30. David Sinclair, "The Invalidity of the Gentile in Agency Law," *HaMishpat HaIvri*, vol. 9 (Jerusalem: Judicial Institute, Hebrew University, 5742-3), p. 100, note 28, and pp. 103–5. Haim Ze'ev Reinas, "The Relations Between Jews and Gentiles in Historic Perspective." Included in a tractate: *Under God's Auspices/Be'Ohaley Ha'Shem* (New York: Newman Publishers, n.d.), pp. 145–77. Ephraim Elimelech Auerbach, *Hazal: Emunot Ve'Deot/The Sages—Beliefs and Opinions* (Jerusalem: Magnes Press, 5729), pp. 480–94. Ze'ev Falk, *Mavo L'Dinei Yisrael B'Yimei HaBayit HaSheyni/Introduction to Jewish Law during the Second Temple Period*, vol. 2 (Tel Aviv: Tel Aviv University Press, 5731), pp. 242–63, especially p. 59–63. Addy Ofir, "Jew-Gentile: A Controversy," *Prosa* 81–82 (Ramat Gan: Melan Press, January 1986), p. 23.

Israeli media disclosed the existence of a blacklist of Jewish landlords who rented their apartments in Jerusalem's Neve Ya'acov neighborhood to Arabs (*Ma'ariv* of 14 January 1986). On Orthodox Jew's seclusion and xenophobia toward non-orthodox Jews, see Rabbi Shaul Yisraeli, "The Beautiful Country," in *Hilchot Eretz Yisrael/The Laws of the Land of Israel* (Jerusalem, 5742), 2nd edition, pp. 42–43. He says, *inter alia*, that an observing Jew is obliged to move to a town having an observing (Orthodox) majority.

55. Basic Law: The Knesset (Amendment No. 9), *ILR*, 1155, p. 196.

56. Penal Law (Amendment No. 20) 5746–1986, *ILR*, 1191, p. 219, 13 August 1986.

57. Rabbi Theodore Friedman, "Halachic Pro . . .," the *Jerusalem Post* of 2 April 1986.

This racist and xenophobic trend does not apply to Rabbi Kahane. Deputy mayor of Jerusalem, Rabbi Nissim Ze'ev (Shas Party), demanded the reconstruction of the Old City of Jerusalem and restriction of the new building to Jews (*Kol HaIr/The Voice of the City*) (weekly) (10 January 1986). This trend affected even the Israeli Army. A military chaplain (an Orthodox rabbi) was investigated by military authorities on charges of incitement to extermination while addressing soldiers as to his spiritual-rabbinic duties (see the *Daily Guardian* of 27 May 1986; *Davar* of 30 May 1986). Eliahu Salpeter, "On Religious Fanaticism in the Israeli Army," *Ha'Aretz* of 2 June 1986. Regarding the specific incident of the military rabbi in charge of Judea and Samaria, the military judge advocate found no foundation to serve a criminal charge, and suggested that more care be taken in wording religious sermons in the future. See also: Yad Vashem staff members' letter against Jewish xenophobia expressed by Kahane MK, in the *Jerusalem Post* of 18 November 1985, and note 33 in Section IV.

58. *Yedioth Aharonoth* of 24 December 1985. See also: *Religious Liberty and the Law*, proceedings of symposia sponsored by the Israel Interfaith Committee, The American Jewish Committee, and the United Christian Council in Israel, 1980. S. Zalman Abramov, *Perpetual Dilemma: Jewish Religion in the Jewish State* (New Jersey: Associated University Press, Inc., 1976). S. Clement Leslie, *The Rift in Israel: Religious Authority and Secular Democracy* (London: Routledge & Kegan Paul Ltd., 1971). Shulamith Aloni, *Nashim K'Bnei Adam/ Women as Human Beings* (Jerusalem: Mabat Publications, 1976) (Hebrew). David H. Ellenson, *Liberal Judaism in Israel: Problems and Prospects* (Los Angeles: Hebrew Union College, n.d.). Alfred Gottschalk (President, Hebrew Union College), "A Strategy for Non-Orthodox Judaism in Israel," *Judaism* (Fall, 1982), p. 421.

59. Reuven Rinsky, "The Problem of Jewish Settlement in Israel and the Zionist Managerial Institutes in the 1920-1930s" (dissertation, Bar Ilan University, Ramat Gan, 5740). Moshe Eshon, "Status Quo-Vadis," *HaZofeh* of 2 March 1984. Jacob Raby, "Another Thought on Secular Shabbat," the *Daily Guardian* of 9 March 1984. Eliezer Don Yehieh, "Division, Denial, and Combination of the Views of Traditional Judaism and Its Ideas on Socialistic Zionism," *Kivunim/Directions* 8 (Jerusalem: The Zionist Movement, 5740), pp. 29–46 and especially note 2. Jacob Katz, "Religion as a United and Separate Power in Modern Jewish History," in *Leumiyut Yehudit-Massoret U'Mechkarim/Jewish Nationalism—Tradition and Research* (Jerusalem: Zionist Press, 5739), pp. 134–36, and also his article "Israeli Society's Jewish Character," p. 106, which is erroneous in preferring Judaism's secularity to secularism that is totally detached from the Jewish understanding and Jewish religious symbols.

Mordecay Levin, *Archei HaChevra V'Calcalah V'HaIdeologia Shel Tekufat*

Ha'Haskala/Social and Economic Values and Ideology of the Age of Enlightenment (Jerusalem: Bialik Institute, 5736). Jacob Shavit, *From Hebrew to Canaanite* (Tel Aviv: Domino Press, 1984), pp. 158–59 (Hebrew). Alexander Altman, *Panim Shel Yehadut/The Face of Judaism* (Tel Aviv: Am-Oved Publishing House, 1983) (Hebrew). Jacob Katz, *Massoret U'Mashber/Tradition and Crisis* (Jerusalem: Bialik Institute, 5718), pp. 302–4. Shmuel Almog, *Zionut V'Historia/Zionism and History*, vol. 9, pp. 137–46 (Jerusalem: Magnes Press, 5742). Meiri Pa'il, "Free Immigration, Jewish State," in the *Daily Guardian* of 11 January 1985.

On the religious status of the State of Israel see: Rabbi Pinhas Palai, "The State of Israel in Light of Jewish Thought," *HaZofeh* of 17 April 1983 and 15 April 1983. Rabbi Shlomo Goren, *Torat HaShabbat V'HaMoed/The Study of Sabbath and Holiday* (Jerusalem, 5742), pp. 455–57. Shlomo Zalman Shraggai, "Prior to Redemption to the Beginning of Redemption," *HaZofeh* of 19 September 1977. Aharon Stritovsky, "The Laws of Independence Day and Jerusalem Day," *Morasha/Heritage* 8, p. 34 (Jerusalem: HaKotel Yeshiva, 5736–July 1976). Uriel Tal, "The Political Messianism in Israel," *Ha'Aretz* of 26 September 1984.

60. Bill concerning Cooperative Associations 5725-1965, *Bills*, 666, p. 306. Bill concerning Cooperative Associations 5725-1968, *Bills*, 778, p. 249, par. 189 and 199.

61. Avigdor Levontin, *Al HaKoshi Lehiyot Yisraeli/On the Difficulty of Being Israeli* (Jerusalem: Van Leer Institute, 1983), p. 43. (Hebrew).

62. Manahem Ron-Wexler, "The Preservation of a Corpse's Skin for Burn Victims," *Assia Book*, vol. 60, (Jerusalem: R. Mass Publications, 5743), pp. 146–248 (Hebrew). M. Z. Cohen, "The Skin of a Corpse and Its Burial Sheets Are Forbidden for Pleasurable Use—Why?" *HaMaor/The Light*, 10th year, issue 10, pp. 4–7. Rabbi Shlomo Goren, "Skin Grafts for Burn Victims in Light of Halacha," *HaZofeh* of 22 March 1985. Kalman Kahane, "On Skin Banks and Skin Grafts," *Ha'Aretz* of 1 April 1985. In opposition to the trend, see Baruch Beraka, "The Spoiled Fruits of the Anatomical Law," *Ha'Aretz* of 18 March 1985. "It is forbidden to transplant Jewish hearts or kidneys," Rabbi Eliezer Yehudah Waldenberg, quoted in *Ma'ariv*, 7 November 1986.

63. Prof. Amnon Rubinstein, "Law and Religion in Israel," *Israel Law Review*, vol. 2, no. 3 (July 1967), p. 381. Amiel Moshe Avigdor, *HaYesodot HaIdeologim Shel HaMizrachi/The Ideological Foundations of Mizrachi* (Warsaw: Mizrachi, 1934). Isaac Brener,"Memorandum on the Attitude of Agudat Yisrael to the Jewish State" and "Program for a United Religious Front on the Question of a Constitution for the Jewish State," ed. Isaac Lewin (New York: Research Institute for Post-War Problems of Religious Jews, 1947). Yosef Talmon, "Coalescence of Socialism with Religion," *Deoth* 40 (Spring 1971).

64. Jacob L. Talmon, *Israel among the Nations* (London: Weidenfeld and Nicolson, 1970, p. 132.

Chapter Three: Quo Vadis Orthodoxy

1. Baruch Na'eh, *Ma'ariv* of 12 March 1984, p. 3.
2. Nurit Amital, *Ha'Aretz* of 11 March 1984, p. 1.
3. Gad Lior, *Yedioth Aharonoth* of 18 April 1984.
4. Yehudah Shalhav and Menahem Friedman, *Hitpashtut Toch Histagrut-Hakihillah HaCharedit B'Yerushalayim/Expansion via Seculsion—The Ultra-Orthodox Community in Jerusalem* (Jerusalem: Jerusalem Institute for Israeli Research, 5746) (Hebrew).
5. Arie Bender, *Ma'ariv* of 13 April 1984.
6. *Ha'Aretz* of 15 June 1984. Shraga Nadav on religious reasoning for sanctions against "hostile Gentile population."
7. For a definition of the term *free* (the Hebrew expression for non-Orthodox), see: "Since a Man Dies, He Is Freed from the Commandments" in *Midrash Tehillim/Collection of Psalms*, 47:88, Buber edition. *Kitzur Bavli/Abridged Babylonian Talmud*, col. 2. *Yalkut Shimoni* (book of legends collected from the Oral Law). *Tractate Shabbat* of *BT*, vol. 30, col. 2. *Tractate Niddah* of *BT*, p. 61, col. 2. Eliezer Ben Yehuda of Jerusalem, *A Complete Dictionary of Ancient and Modern Hebrew* (New York and Berlin: Langenscheidt, 1944), vol. 3, p. 1697, *s.v.* "Hofshi" (free, colorless, weak).
8. Kach movement advertisement (undated): "Daughter of Israel! You are the daughter of a large, chosen and extraordinary nation. Please do not defile yourself. Do not disgrace yourself. Do not go out with Arabs and other Gentiles. You need not be "religious" in order to understand how great and important it is to be a proud Jewish woman. You need not be "religious" to understand that your children, and theirs, must be the continuation of generations of the Jewish People. Beware of the Arab who wants to disgrace and insult you. Daughter of Israel, date only Sons of Israel! And Sons of Israel, you are being called upon to join the "protectors of Jewish honor" by helping. The protectors will take upon themselves the role of preventing the drowning and assimilation of Jews. The activities of the protectors will be legal and in accordance with the police. Join now . . . ."
9. A citizen who led to the arrest and conviction, in the Civil Court, of an ultra-Orthodox man, claimed to have been harassed by threatening phone calls. He states (*Ma'ariv*, 1 June 1986): "Since I caught a rabbi, my life has become a nightmare."

Interior Minister Yitzhak Peretz (leader of the Shas—Torah Guardians, or religious Sephardic—party) proposed a bill according to which rabbis would enjoy immunity from any matter dealing with criminal offenses they might be suspected of ex officio.

Religious violence is not an extraordinary phenomenon in Israel, but it inevitably has defined aims, which are set in gear every year, usually at the outset of summer. Jerusalem Mayor Teddy Kollek admits that religious violence is not a "static" phenomenon. He feels it is a civil disobedience that gains strength as a result of the "authorities' silence." (See the *Daily Guardian* of 11 June 1986.)

Ultra-Orthodox Interior Minister, Yitzhak Peretz, announced that "we [are in the midst] of a great cultural war" (*Ma'ariv* of 11 June 1986), while Chief Rabbi Mordechai Eliahu attacked the government of Israel, during the peak of ultra-Orthodox violence (igniting bus stop shelters throughout the country, Sabbath rallies in Petach Tikva), when he awarded an ethical validation to his followers, and called upon the government to "repent" (*Ma'ariv* of 11 June 1986).

The ideologic view resulting in the wave of violence is evident. The conduct of the common Israeli is despised and loathed. See *Ma'ariv* of 8 June 1986, in which an ultra-Orthodox rabbi stated that the injury caused to the souls of religious Jews from the "atrocious advertisements" pasted on the bus stop shelters is as bad as the harm done by the nuclear plant in Chernobyl. Prime Minister Shimon Peres also admitted that the religious violence is a phenomenon the government lacks the tools to fight as a result of the political aspect of the violence (*Hadashot/News* of 16 June 1986). It is worthwhile to note that the civil disobedience of summer 1986 alone necessitated 2,400 workdays by Jerusalem police (*Kol Yerushalayim* of 12 June 1986). This is not meant to point to the effectiveness of the police. On the contrary, the results are insufficient. Police intelligence is not successful at penetrating the militant religious groups; the percentage of solved crimes committed by the ultra-Orthodox is miniscule. Also, we cannot ignore the political factor with which the security forces must deal. The result is a sense of victory among the ultra-Orthodox (*Yedioth Aharonoth* of 11 June 1986).

A group of ultra-Orthodox zealots prevented construction of a hotel by exercising physical and economic pressure. Finally, a compromise was reached— that is, the so-called "moderate" Orthodox establishment agreed to the major ultra-Orthodox demands, paying lip service to the rule of law (*Ha'Aretz* of 3 February 1984).

Professor Uzi Ornan, one of the past leaders of the groups active in the struggle against religious coercion, stated that "only when the ultra-Orthodox are beaten up do they feel exempt from [fulfilling] the commandments of war against secularists . . ." (*Kol Ha'Ir/The City's Voice* of 20 June 1986).

Dov Tabori, mayor of the town of Petach Tikva, expressed helplessness against religious violence, stating: "I did not surrender; but for how long can I listen as they proposition my daughter to work as a prostitute?"

10. "Treaty" between the ultra-Orthodox factions to prevent internal terrorism (*Davar* of 30 May 1986), while the ultra-Orthodox struggle amongst themselves to prevent the construction of a yeshiva by an Orthodox group other

than their own (*Kol Yerushalayim* of 20 June 1986).

11. Regarding the Sabbath rallies in Jerusalem during the 1930s and the struggles against religious coercion led by the League against Religious Coercion, see Arie Dayan, "Religious Wars in Israel" (three-part article), *Kol Ha'Ir* of 26 August 1983, 3 September 1982, and 10 September 1982. See also Levy Yitzhak HaYerushalmi, *Ma'ariv* of November 1963.

12. High Court of Justice (Supreme Court) 174/62, the League against Religious Coercion v. Jerusalem Municipality *ILR*, vol. 37, p. 2665.

13. Survey by Smith Institute taken on request of the Jerusalem Municipality (*Davar* of 25 May 1986) states that 66 percent of the non-Orthodox Jerusalemites foresee deterioration in relations with the Orthodox.

14. On the tendency of religious Judaism to isolate itself from secular society, see Rabbi Shaul Yisraeli, "The Beautiful Country," in *Hilchot Eretz Yisrael/ The Laws of the Land of Israel,* 2nd ed., pp. 42–43, which deals with settling in the land of Israel. When a person from Israel has not the opportunity to settle amidst those who keep the commandments, as opposed to "those who are rotted," that person should move to a city where most of the inhabitants are "legitimate," i.e., secular. Maimonides, *Hilkhot De'ot,* pp. 6311. See also *Gemara Appendix: Tosephet L'Hagigah/Appendix to the Festivity,* 27 col. A, *s.v.* "poshei'a," (criminal). Akkiba Eldar, "The Ultra-Orthodox in Israel—Them and Us" and "The Struggle for the Boundaries of Settlement," *Ha'Aretz* of 5 April 1983.

In halachic literature see, *inter alia*: Rabbi Shmuel Shmellka from Nicklsburg, *Sefer Divrey Shmuel/The Writings of Shmuel* (Jerusalem: Mussar Ve'Hassidut Publishers, n.d.), par. 63. Rabbi Joseph Caro's *Shulhan Arukh: Orakh Haim,* par. 12, and *Shulhan Arukh: Yoreh Deah,* par. 1 and par. 219. Rabbi Uri Dassberg, "The criteria for Division of Public Monies," *Tehumin,* vol. 4 (Alon Shevut: Zomet Publications, 5743), p. 413 and notes 82 and 83. Joseph Foyer, *Iyunim B'Mishneh Torah L'Rambam/Studies in Maimonides' Mishneh Torah* (Jerusalem: Ha'Rav Kook Publications, 5738), pp. 250–51 and note 27.

15. Maimonides, *Hilkhot Evel/The Laws of Mourning,* par. 14, based on *Tractate Pessahim* of the *BT,* 203, col. 2. Compare with Maimonides, *Hilkhot Rotze'ach U'Shmirat HaNefesh/The Laws Regarding Murderers and Preservation of the Soul,* par. 13: "Your brother—in commandments, and since he dies he becomes freed from the commandments and once again is not a brother." Avraham Sherman, "The Relationship of Halacha toward Our Brothers Who Have Left the Way of Torah and Commandments," *Tehumin,* vol. A (Alon Shevut: Zomet Publications, 5730), pp. 311–13. Shalom Rosenberg, "You Walked in His Path," *Philosophia Yisraelit/Israeli Philosophy* (Tel Aviv: Papyrus Publications, Tel Aviv University, 5743), p. 75 and especially note 12, and p. 74. Moshe Yehudai, "The Worth of the Life of a Non-Jew in Halacha" (dissertation submitted to the Hebrew University of Jerusalem, 5743), p. 124 and note 74.

ET, vol. I, *s.v.* "ach" (brother), pp. 202–3. Shlomo Goren, *Torat HaMoadim/ The Study of the Seasons* (Tel Aviv, 5724), pp. 43ff. On the problem of accepting the secularists as "brothers" in our time, see Menahem Rackman, "Mutual Unity and Appreciation," *HaZofeh* of 7 September 1983.

16. Avraham Sherman, "The Relationship of Halacha Toward Our Brothers Who Have Left the Way of Torah and Commandments," *Tehumin*, vol. B (Alon Shevut: Zomet Publications, 5731), pp. 267–71.

17. On the problem of serving food in the kibbutz dining hall for someone who does not make the necessary blessings or for a person who does not ritually wash his hands, including the prohibition of feeding (since it is considered to come under the halacha, "Do not put an obstacle in front of a blind man") see: Rabbi Shlomo Aviner, *Am K'laviah*, vol. A (Jerusalem, 5743), pp. 334–35, par. 465 and 466, who permits giving food since "he might become enraged and hateful against all those following the way of the Torah." For permission to sell food to those who do not ritually wash their hands or make the blessing, see: Rabbi Eliezer Judah Waldenberg, *Responsa Tzitz Eliezer* (Jerusalem: private publication, 5738) (16 volumes of monumental contemporary ḥalachic research). See, *inter alia*, vol. 5, or patients visiting (including restrictions on Sabbath), vols. 7, 8, 11, on plates, food, and cooking in which Gentiles are involved.

Rabbi Shlomo Oyerbach, *Minhat Shlomo* (Jerusalem: Shaarey Ziv Publishers, 5746), par.: 35, pp. 189–90.

18. See note 14, above.

19. Criminal Files 3471–2/87. The Jerusalem Municipal Court. Verdict unpublished. See also: Moshe Negbi, *On the Freedom of Conscience, Religion, and Culture* (interpretation of the verdict of Judge Ayalah Proccacia on movies on Sabbath) (Jerusalem: Hemdat, 1988) (foreword by former Justice Haim Cohen) (Hebrew).

20. Major Shalit's case. High Court of Justice 58/68, *ILR*, vol. 23(2), p. 608.

21. Amendment to the Law of Return, 14 March 1970. *ILB*, 568, p. 34.

22. Municipal Authorities Act (Special Authorization), 5722–1962, ILB, 317, p. 106.

23. *Ma'alit Otomatit B'Shabbat/An Automatic Sabbath Elevator* (Jerusalem: Institute for Technological Sciences and Questions of Halacha, 5729), and *Hashmal B'Halacha/Electricity in Halacha*, vol. A (Jerusalem: Institute for Technological Sciences and Questions of Halacha, 5738), p. 303ff, and vol. B (Jerusalem: Institute for Technological Sciences and Questions of Halacha, 5741), pp. 329ff. Also, "Electricity and the Sabbath" is the bibliographical compilation (Jerusalem: Institute for Technological Sciences and Questions of Halacha, 5735), pp. 141ff.

24. On the special telephone designed for use on the Sabbath, see: *Responsa: Deeds of Thought*, vol. A (Jerusalem: Institute for Technological Sciences and

Questions of Halacha, 5745 (pp. 53–103, which deals with a "Sabbath-phone" allowing incoming calls in accordance with halacha).

25. See Rabbi Yitzhak Ya'acov Weiss, *Responsa: Minchat Yitzhak*, part A, par. 53; part 3, par. 20, letters 6–10. Rabbi Joseph Caro's *Shulhan Arukh: Yoreh De'ah, Responsa* 154. Rabbi Moshe Isserles, known as "The Diaspora Fountain" (Beer Ha'Golah), interpretation of the *Shulhan Arukh: Orakh Hayim. Mishnah Brura*, part 329, sub-par. 9 and par. 385 (c) states that a man who performs transgressions for the purpose of provoking anger cannot be rescued (divinely forgiven) during weekdays, but even more so, it is forbidden to desecrate the Sabbath for him (vol. 3 and vol. 4 dealing with Sabbath restrictions) (New York: Joseph Sachs Publishers, 1943). See also: Harry Neubort, *Halacha V'Rifuah/Halacha and Medicine*, vol. A, p. 160. Maimonides, *Hilchot Evel*, part A. Haim David HaLevi, *A'seh Lecha Rav* (Tel Aviv: Dvir Publications, 5743), pp. 212–21, on the laws and discussions of mourning for those who have left the way of the public. Rabbi Moshe Hershler, ed., *Halakha and Medicine*. A symposium, vol. 1 and vol. 2. (Jerusalem-Chicago: Regensberg Institute, 5740–1980), *inter alia*: vol. 1: Rabbi Ovadia Yosef, *Treating a non-Jewish patient on Sabbath*, pp. 147–150. vol. 2: *Sabbath in Medicine*; Rabbi Yehoshua Neuwirth, *Performing Arts Prohibited on Sabbath by Means of a Gentile*, pp. 199–204. Dr. Mayer Issacson, *Halachic Problems Involved in Diagnosing and Preventing Infections on Sabbath*, pp. 252–54.

26. Rabbi Eliezer Yehudah Waldenberg, *Responsa Tzitz Eliezer*, vols. 7, 8, 10, and 11.

27. Rabbi Yitzhak Yacob Weiss: *Responsa Minhat Yitzhak (On Jewish Doctors' Duties, sign 53, p. 108)*. par. 53 and par. 20 (Tel Aviv: Kfar Habad Lod, 5729–1969). *Yoreh De'ah* in Rabbi Caro's *Shulhan Arukh*, par. 158. On the term "hatred" see *ET*, vol. 1, *s.v.* "ayyah" (hatred), pp. 228–30.

28. Rabbi Yehoshua Neuwirt, *Traveling for Sick Persons on Sabbath*, dealing also with duties to save life on Sabbath of a Gentile and of a Jewish apostate, pp. 160–65, vol. 1.

29. Avraham Sherman, "Saving of Life on the Sabbath, Those Who Have left the Path of Torah," *Tehumin*, vol. C (Alon Shevut: Zomet Publications, 5742), pp. 24–29 and especially p. 27.

30. The disappearance of a patient from Shaare Zedek Hospital as publicized in the press: *Yedioth Aharonoth* of 5 March 1984; *Ma'ariv* of 7 March 1984 and 8 March 1984; *Kol Yerushalayim* of 9 March 1984.

Rabbi Eliezer Yehudah Waldenberg, *Responsa Tzitz Eliezer*, vol. 8, par. 15, chap. 9, includes expressions of some understanding toward the psychological needs of a patient contradicting Sabbath restrictions.

31. Tenth Knesset Resolution, 3 January 1984, *R. K. P.*, vol. 12, pp. 951–57.

32. Under ultra-Orthodox pressure the Jerusalem Gerard Behar's Hall

cancelled a theatrical performance: *Kol Yerushalayim* of 30 August 1985. See also: Chief Rabbinate pressure canceled a performance in Caesar's Hall in Jerusalem. Jerusalem supplement of the *Jerusalem Post*, Feb. 5, 1988.

33. Letter by David Ben-Gurion of 24 April 1949 addressed to Rabbi Yitzhak Meir Levin of the Agudat Yisrael accepting some Orthodox coercive demands.

This document is commonly regarded as the first "Status Quo" agreement.

Coalition agreement regarding religious matters during the term of the Second Knesset (January 1953).

Agreement between the Minister of Education and the Minister of Religion of 21 Shvat 5714, with the establishment of a government headed by Moshe Sharett.

Coalition agreement of the Sharett government of 25 January 1954.

Agreement regarding religion and education with the convening of the Third Knesset, as read from the Knesset platform by David Ben-Gurion on 3 November 1955 (RKP, vol. 19, p. 284).

Agreement regarding religion, following elections to the Fourth Knesset, discussed as a letter from Ben-Gurion to Moshe Haim Shapira (4 January 1960).

Coalition agreement regarding education and religion, following elections to the Fifth Knesset (20 October 1961).

Coalition agreement of 11 January 1966 (published in newspapers) (Sixth Knesset).

I was unsuccessful in uncovering coalition documents during the term of the Seventh Knesset (the Labor-Alignment party) or the Ninth Knesset (first term of the Likkud party).

Coalition agreement of the Tenth Knesset between the Likkud party and the religious factions (National Religious Party, Agudat Yisrael, and Tami parties) of 4 August 1981.

34. Criminal file 615/83, State of Israel v. Moshe Hirsch. Magistrate Court of Jerusalem (unpublished). Rabbi Hirsch was suspected of stating "that the flags flown [on Independence Day] are blue and white rags." Rabbi Hirsch was tried for making this statement published in a local newspaper, *Kol Ha'Ir*, as this is a violation of the Law of the Flag and Symbols, which states (par. 5): "One who injures the honor of the State flag or the honor of a State symbol or who causes injury to the honor or uses it in such a way as to injure its honor, is sentenced to a maximum of one year imprisonment and fine."

The Court was consulted on the constitutional problem involved in this matter. In the United States, for example, freedom of expression is anchored in the written constitution. One cannot be punished for a violation, based on a form of expression, committed against a state flag, as harsh as that expression may be. Freedom of expression, which is a constitutional principle, is of the utmost importance. In Israel there is no written constitution or priority for freedom of expression (Additional Hearing 91/77—Electric Company v. *Ha'Aretz, ILR* 32 (4), p. 337). The Jerusalem Court decided to adopt the constitutional principle of freedom of expression, regardless of the absence of a written constitution, and reduced the definition of "Law of the Flag" such that it does not prohibit making statements against the State flag. Freedom of expression was granted preference by the judiciary and the accused was acquitted of causing injury to the flag although the accusation was found to be true.

35. Gad Beliatansky, *Kol Yerushalayim* of 27 January 1984.

36. Civil Service Act (categorizing political party activities and collection of funds) 5719–1959, *ILB*, 289, p. 190.

37. Interview with journalist Zvi Barel in *Ha'Aretz* of 2 March 1984.

38. Law of Public Education 5713–1953, *ILB*, 131, p. 137. Published on 20 August 1953, it was enforced immediately, to enable the start of the 1953–4 academic year as per its instructions.

39. The heads of the Progressive party and its successors, the Independent Liberal party, so identified with the law and were so convinced of the sovereignty it represented that they did not forget to recall "their achievement" at every opportunity as proof of their view and as a sign of things to come.

40. Orit Ichilov, *The Political World of Children and Youth* (Tel Aviv: Yachdav Publishers, 1984) (Hebrew).

41. Rabbi Moshe Zemer, "Hatred of Foreigners—Xenophobia—Hatred of Gentiles—Was in the Last Few Years a Common Phenomenon in Israel," *Ha'Aretz* of 13 April 1984. Addy Ophir, "Jew, Sons of Polemic Writings," *Prose* (January 1986), 81–82, pp. 23ff. Jacob Katz, *Between Jews and Gentiles* (Jerusalem: Bialik Institute, 5721).

42. Zvi Rosenberg, ed., "Joseph Cherishes the Sabbath" (taken from the *Stories of Our Sages*) (Bnei Brak: Sharsheret Books, n.d.).

43. Avraham Schwartz is a past student of Toldot Aharon yeshiva who appeared on a television interview with Ram Evron on "Zeh HaZman" broadcast on 28 May 1984.

44. "Zarkor," the newspaper for the young, #29 issue 684, vol. 18. Blue edition: Independence Day 5742–1987 (For public-religious schools). Green edition: The description "Independence Day" deleted for "Independent" ultra religious schools. Both editions recommended by the Israeli Ministry for Education.

45. Law of Public Education 5713–1953, *ILB*, 131, p. 137. Published on 20 August 1953, it was enforced immediately, to enable the start of the 1953–4 academic year as per its instructions.

46. In the branch of state religious education the idea of separating boys from girls and preventing meetings between Jews and Arabs is crystallizing. The meetings with secular Jewish youth as well are not to be taken lightly. In the Council for Religious Education, the statutory body for public education, a proposition was raised forbidding joint work camps for religious and secular youth, co-ed swimming, and the holding of dances. It was also proposed that

a special role be given to the local rabbi in deciding norms for the meetings between young men and women at dialogues sponsored by the state religious schools (*Ha'Aretz* of 23 May 1986 and 19 June 1986).

47. The Council for Religious Education ordered the cessation of work by a female teacher employed within the framework of state religious education after discovering that her husband publicly desecrates the Sabbath by not wearing a yarmulke and by turning on lights in their home on the Sabbath (*Ha'Aretz* of 18 June 1986).

48. "TALI" (an abbreviation for the Hebrew term "Tochnit l'ha'amakat toda'ah Yehudit" or Program for Jewish Awareness) was accepted in certain secular public schools to introduce religious rituals and religious standards of behavior. This program is subject to parental consent. Several methods were used in this program. Entire lessons dealing with reform and other non-Orthodox religious Jewish ways of life were rejected under this program; however, it is supported by the Conservative Religious Movement in Israel. In addition, Orthodox rabbis are hired to introduce Orthodox theology in public-secular schools (Eleventh Knesset, Parliamentary Commission for Education, session 102, 23 December 1985). In this context, Zionist means secular, and Jewish-Zionist signifies Zionist Religious Orthodoxy (U.H.).

49. Nili Mendlow, *Ha'Aretz* of 4 May 1984.

50. In 1963 a worried parent wrote to the newspaper *HaBoker/Morning* (9 June 1963) asking: "Why aren't the pupils categorized such that those coming from religious homes will not be influenced by children whose parents are secular" (and who study in state religious schools—U.H.). See also *Ha'Aretz* of 29 March 1984 and 12 April 1984, which stated, "The Bilu religious school in Tel Aviv has undergone a process of extremism, while opposing teachers, students, and parents, and has begun a process of separating the sexes (boys and girls are about to start learning in separate schools)."

51. The Movement for Jewish Tradition (Tami) aids Parents' Committees to prevent the change of public religious schools into public ultra-Orthodox schools (*Ha'Aretz* of 23 March 1984).

52. Citizenship Classes in the Public and Public-religious Schools (proposition), 1st edition (Jerusalem: Ministry of Education and Culture, 5736). Even on subjects concerning constitutional values, the curriculum in the two public school systems is different.

53. Law of Equal Opportunity in Work, 5741–1981, *ILB*, 1026, p. 285, states in par. 1: "One who needs an employee will not refuse to receive a person to work or to be sent for training . . . because of sex, marital status, or being a parent." On the other hand, it is not considered discriminatory when the character or essence of a job, or security matters, prevent hiring a member of one of the sexes. However, with regard to lifestyle, the law overlooks wide loopholes filled with discrimination. It is sufficient to scan the job advertisements to see

that many institutes desire a "religious" secretary, "religious" director, "religious" educator, etc. Since the lifestyle of the religious Orthodox flow is no less important to them than their philosophic view, the discrimination can no longer be based on ideology. Focusing on a specific lifestyle is enough to cause discrimination between one citizen and another with regard to employment. This is the situation faced by those accepting jobs that require them to work on the Sabbath as well as workers who are willing to work on the Sabbath but whose potential employers forbid such work. In any event, there still remains a large difference between the two types of discrimination; religious (Orthodox) employees will be denied the job due to their refusal to work on the Sabbath and holidays; however, nobody would investigate their philosophical views if, despite lifestyle, they chose to accept a position that obligated them to be on duty on days of rest. This is not the case with the Orthodox institution, which stipulates that the employment of workers depends on their being "religious" within their homes as well as outside their place of employment; subservience to the "religious" norms only while at work is not sufficient for the "religious" employer.

54. Rabbi Moshe Zvi Neriah in *Ma'ariv* of 28 May 1963. Rabbi Shlomo Goren, *Torah HaShabbat ViHaMoed/ The Study of Torah, the Sabbat and the Seasons* (Jerusalem: Jewish Agency, Dept. for Toraic Culture, 5732), pp. 419–31, 432–46) (Hebrew). Rabbi Shlomo Goren, "Laws of State in Israel," in *Shanah B'Shana*, 5735, pp. 127–35. Rabbi Shlomo Goren, "The Commandments between a Person and the State," *HaZofeh* of 24 September 1976. Danny Rubinstein, *Me, LaShem Elay—Gush Emunim/ Who is for My God, Join Me—Gush Emunim* (Tel Aviv: Hakibbutz HaMeuchad Publishing House Ltd., 5742–1982) (Hebrew). Gaby Oren, "Eretz Yisrael between Religion and Politics" (survey) (Jerusalem: Jerusalem Institute for Israeli Research, 1985), no. 18; Ehud Sprinzak, *Gush Emunim—The Politics of Zionist Fundamentalism in Israel* published by The American Jewish Committee, 1986. Amnon Rubinstein, *Me-Herzl Ad Gush Emunim V'Chazara/ From Herzl to Gush Emunim and Back* (Tel Aviv: Shocken Press, 1980) (Hebrew).

On the trend of giving a redeemed mystical reason for the existence of the State of Israel, see: Shlomo Zalman Shraggai, "From the Beginning of Redemption to the Start of the Growth of Redemption," *HaZofeh* of 12 September 1977. Eliezer Don-Yihieh, "Views of Zionism," *Ma'asef HaZiyonut/ The Zionist*, vol. 9 (Tel Aviv: Tel Aviv University Press, 5744), p. 85. "Zionism and Its Opponents, Tradition and Modernization, Messianism and Romanticism," *Zmanim/ Times* 14 (Tel Aviv: Tel Aviv University Press, Winter 1984), p. 64. Rabbi Pinchas Pla'i, "Religious Dimensions in the State of Israel" (Jerusalem: Association for Jewish Consciousnes, 5731), p. 33. Rabbi Pinchas Pla'i, "The Jewish State in Light of Jewish Thought," *HaZofeh* of 17 April 1983, which diagnoses three views: prophetic, midrashic (oral law), and halachic. Rabbi Shlomo Goren, "The Cities of Judah and the Cities of Israel in Light of Halacha,"

HaZofeh of 3 August 1984. Rabbi Israel Shchipansky, "The Commandment of Settling the Land of Israel Today," *Shana B'Shana* (yearbook) (Jerusalem: Heichal Shlomo, 5745), pp. 209–13. Rabbi Zvi Yehudah HaCohen Kook, *Netivot Yisrael/Paths of Israel*, vol. 1 (Jerusalem: Barei HaAretz Publications, 1984), p. 122. Rabbi Zvi Raanan, *Gush Emunim* (Tel Aviv: Sifriat Poalim Publishers, 1980). Janet O'Dea, "Gush Emunim: Roots and Ambiguities—The Perspective of the Sociology of Religion" *Forum* No. 2 (25), (Jerusalem: World Zionist Organization, 1976), pp. 39–50.

55. Rabbi Avraham Semel is the Chief Rabbi of the Israel Defense Forces Central Command (Res.). In his article "The Purity of Weapons in Light of Halacha" in *B'Ikvot Milhemet Yom HaKippurim—Pirkei HaGut, Halachi U'Mehkar/After the Yom Kippur War—Expressions, Halacha, and Research* (Jerusalem: Office of the Military Rabbinate, Central Command, 5734), pp. 26–31, he determines "that in any event, one must not trust an Arab, even when he gives the impression of being a man of culture."

Rabbi Eliezer Waldenberg stated that it is forbidden for Gentiles to be a majority in Israeli cities. He is a recipient of the Israel Prize for Jewish Thought, and neither the judges nor the Minister of Education and Culture (the Parliamentary representative for the awarding of this prize) thought to question the choice of prizewinner despite his beliefs.

56. Rabbi Yisrael Ariel, whose name appeared on a declaration bearing Rabbi Meir Kahane's picture, and who is identified with him, stated: "There is only one Israel, from the Nile River to the Euphrates River. The entire land belongs to the People of Israel and there is no room for Gentiles." (These declarations were also made by Kahane in *Ma'ariv* of 12 June 1981). Ariel continued: "I am not separating from my friends in the National Religious Party— a group among the best in the country which did not win the leadership which it would carry out based upon the Torah." He closed, "This time, Kahane— vote Kach."

A member of a Jewish terrorist group was released from prison and escorted by police to Hebron where his wedding was to be held. The ceremony took place at the Tomb of the Patriarchs and turned into a rally of hundreds of settlers supporting those arrested members of the underground. Rabbi Yisrael Ariel performed the wedding and blessed those arrested. See also *Yedioth Aharonoth* of 13 June 1984.

57. It is worthwhile to emphasize that in the eyes of the non-nationalistic Orthodox Jews, attempts to pray on temple Mount, the destruction of the mosques, and the construction of the Temple are seen as acts of heresy. The original Orthodox understanding of halacha forbids a Jew from entering the area of Temple Mount, since one must not accelerate nor precipitate the end of days nor speed the coming of the redemption. According to this understanding, the activities of the nationalist religious Jews bring about the breaking of the

yoke of commandments of blood desecration. But some highly motivated and intelligent members of the nationalist Orthodoxy rejected this ultra-Orthodox theology, introducing the contrasting ideology of Greater Israel and Jewish religious presence on the Temple Mount.

Avraham Ahituv, the former commander of Israel's General Security Forces (the Shin Bet), warned that the Jewish settlers in the West Bank (Judea and Samaria) were "a hatching ground for terrorism," based on messianic religious ideology. This group of settlers and their followers received political and moral support from religious-Orthodox and secular rights leaders. Chief (Orthodox) Rabbi Mordekhai Eliahu and the Deputy Speaker of the Knesset, Meir Cohen-Avidor, MK (Likud), collected money for families of the accused, some from Jewish communities in the United States; Yitzhak Shamir, then-Deputy Prime Minister, attended a rally and remained silent when settler leaders warned that any decision to surrender part of the West Bank would be considered by them as illegal (the *Jerusalem Post* of 18 March 1985).

The intention of "purifying the Temple Mount from Moslem possession, in order to bring about the redemption of Israel and the establishment of the promised kingdom of Israel" was one of the principal aims disclosed by one of the members of the alleged Jewish underground (the *Jerusalem Post*, 4 June 1984; *Hadashot*, 11 March 1987).

58. *HaShofar/The Ram's Horn* 2 (house organ of the "Hasmonean Youth" Organization).

59. Joel Lerner, *Ha'Aretz* of 25 May 1984. The Rishon LeZion of Chief Rabbi Mordekhai Eliyahu, "A Jewish Synagogue Must Be Erected on the Southeastern or Northeastern Slope of the Temple Mount," *Yedioth Aharonoth*, 31 January 1986.

60. Joel Lerner wrote to me, in a letter of 18 March 1985, "You demand that I educate all Jewish youth to the Jewish reality in which women serve as priests and which fundamentally erases the prayer 'Thank God for not making me a woman.' I am sorry to say that it is difficult for me to agree with you on this point: there is no *Judaism* [emphasis in orginal] which behaves this way, although there are *Jews* [emphasis in original] who behave this way, but, in actuality, they are not Judaism . . ."

61. "Temple Mount Fundamentalists Launching New Mideast Holy Wars," *Executive Intelligence Review*, 26 April 1983. Hagay Segal, *Dear Brothers—The Jewish Underground Story* (Jerusalem: Keter Publishing House, 1987) (Hebrew).

62. The Israel Defense Forces captured huge amounts of explosives and weapons. Among other things, 32 hand grenades, 113 mines, 8 explosive devices, 12 submachine guns, and large quantities of dynamite were discovered. It must be emphasized that the Jewish settlers were also armed with "official" weapons supplied to them by the Defense Forces themselves for the purpose of self-defense, in its contained legal definition.

63. The *Jerusalem Post* of 11 May 1984, an interview with Rabbi Z. M. Neriah. *Ma'ariv*, 13 May 1984, Zvi Barel, "Two Types of Ethics." *Ha'Aretz*, 24 May 1984.

64. The convention was held in Jerusalem under the initiative of the Netivot Shalom (Paths of Peace) and Oz Shalom (Peaceful Strength) movements, which express a modern religious-Orthodox philosophy advocating peaceful political solution along with the Arabs based on mutual compromise. Rabbi Yehudah Amital, a prominent Orthodox theologian and head of Yeshiva College, is affiliated with these movements. In an interview to the press he expressed his opinion concerning democracy in Israel. He stated: "The Declaration of Independence obligates from a halachic point of view" (*Hadashot*, 4 June 1986). By making this statement, Rabbi Amital legitimized the existing constitutional structure of Israel, parting from many of his Orthodox colleagues.

On the recognition of a merger between secular law and halacha in Israel and the conflict between them, see editorials in *HaZofeh* of 19 August 1981 and 2 October 1981. Also see: Eliezer Berkowitz, "Religious Coercion—Is It in Accordance with Halacha?," *Ma'ariv* of 28 September 1981, which points to the halachic system's dependency on the rule of State.

On the denial of halacha as a decisive element in Israel, see editorial in *Ha'Aretz* of 22 September 1981. Also, Haim Zadok, "Halacha Does Not Govern Our Way of Life," *Ma'ariv* of 2 October 1980. (Former Minister of Justice) Jacob Rabi, "Law and Halacha—Exact Expressions," the *Daily Guardian* of 9 October 1981.

65. Yitzhak Gruenbaum, *Ma'ariv* of 25 March 1964. (Gruenbaum was one of the most prominent leaders of Polish Jewry until World War II and a member of the Polish Parliament. He became the first Israeli Cabinet Minister for Interior Affairs.)

Chapter Four: The Place Where They Must Take You In

1. The Law of Return, 5710–1950 in *ILB*, 51, p. 159, of 6 July 1950; and amendment 5730 in same, 586, p. 34, of 14 March 1970.

2. "Who is a Jew," *Ha'Aretz* of 3 January 1965, statement by Minister Moshe Haim Shaprio.

3. Civil File 419/64, Ilana Stern v. State of Israel, Jerusalem District Court (unpublished).

4. Governmental decision, 1 July 1958 (13 Tammuz 5718).

5. High Court of Justice, Jerusalem (Supreme Court) File 72/62, Oswald Ruffeisen v. Minister of the Interior, *ILR*, vol. 17, p. 2428.

6. On Judaism's understanding as a subjective expression see: Eliezer Schweid, "The Position and Value of the Single Person," *Da'at/Knowledge* (Ramat Gan: Bar Ilan University, 5733), pp. 91–101, especially 95–96. Baruch Kurzweil, "New Jewish Thought," *Ha'Aretz* of 11 January 1945.

7. Benjamin Zvielli, "Are We Not Hellenized," *HaZofeh* of 17 December 1982. Shmuel Almog, *Zionut V'Historia/Zionism and History* (Jerusalem: Magnes Press, 5732–1982), p. 92, note 45 (Hebrew). Ehud Luz, *Makbilim Nifgashim/Parallels Meet* (Tel Aviv: Am-Oved Publishing House, Ofakkim Series, 1985), pp. 123–30 and 134–37.

8. Jacob Shavit, *M'Ivri Ad Canaanite/From Hebrew to Canaanite* (Tel Aviv University: Domino Press, 1984). Jacob Katz, "Zionism and Jewish Awareness" in *HaLeumiyut HaYehudit/Jewish Nationalism* (Jerusalem: The Zionist Library, 5739), p. 78.

9. Joseph Power, *Iyunim BaMishneh Torah L'Rambam/Studies in Maimonides' Mishneh Torah* (Jerusalem: HaRav Kook Publications, 5738), pp. 250–51, and note 29.

10. Gershon Weiler, *HaTeocratia HaYehudit/Jewish Theocracy* (Tel Aviv: Am-Oved Publishing House, 5732–1977).

11. The main relevant acts of the Knesset concerning this subject are the Law of Return and the laws regarding the Population Registry.

In the original legislation—the Law of Return as accepted by the Knesset in 1950—there was no strict definition of "who is a Jew." The original ordinance for the Population Registry (1949) gave no powers whatsoever to the government authorities (specifically the Ministry of the Interior) to restrict registration of new emigrants declaring bona fide their national (ethnic) origin as well as their religious creed.

Thus, room was left for various interpretations regarding the sensitive subject of Jewishness as far as the citizenship of newcomers was concerned. The Ministry of the Interior from time to time issued "internal office directives." (For the Shalit case, see *ILR*, 23 (2), pp. 509, 515, 517.)

The "directives" were never published and could not be, by any means, considered as secondary legislation, such as bylaws or regulations. The "directives" were subject to changes according to political-ideological changes in the Ministry of the Interior.

Until 1958—mainly under a socialist Minister of the Interior—the directive was to register almost every newcomer as a Jew without investigation as long as his or her declaration could be considered bona fide.

As an unusual step, on 20 July 1958 the government itself was involved in approving a directive issued by the Ministry of the Interior that reads: ". . . to register as a Jew every person who declares his Jewishness bona fide and *does not belong to any other religious denomination*." For the first time, Jewish nationality and religious affiliation were combined by the Israeli secular administrative body.

On January 1, 1960, the following directive was issued by the Ministry of the Interior:

> Children born as a result of mixed relations to be registered as following regarding "religion" and "nationality":
>
> (a) Children born to a Jewish mother and to a Gentile father to be registered as "Jew" by both nationality and religion.
>
> (b) Children born to a Jewish father and to a Gentile mother to be registered (regarding both nationality and religion) following the mother's description in this regard.
>
> In case of parents' refusal to act as mentioned above, the children to be registered following the non-Jewish religious and national connection submitted by the parents.
>
> In case of parents' refusal of the above-mentioned option, or while the parents did not submit any non-Jewish option concerning religion and nationality, the registration to be executed as follows:
>
> (1) father—Jewish
> mother—Gentile
>
> (2) The detail "nationality" not to be fulfilled in the questionnaire or in the identity card.
>
> Proved that the children duly converted to Judaism following an authorized Religious Tribunal decision, to be registered as "Jew" regarding both nationality and religion.

Simultaneously, legal precedents as well as changes in the Law of Return and the Law concerning Population Registry created the status quo described in detail in this book.

12. See note 5 above.

13. Cabinet Minister of Interior, as quoted in Ruffeisen case (note 5 above).

14. Shulamit Aloni in *Yedioth Aharonoth* of 23 August 1984.

15. Enrico Ricardetto, *Epoca* no. 646, 10 February 1963 (Roma) (Italian).

16. Jacob Meron in *Ha'Aretz* of 30 October 1969.

17. Prof. Avraham Yehoshua Heschel, response of 18 December 1958 to David Ben-Gurion's address on the issue of "who is a Jew." Especially noteworthy are the Polish sources regarding preservation of the national ethnic identity. See: Adam Jaworski, *Kultura* (Paris: Instytut Literacki, 1957), vol. 6/16. Hippolit Olgard Buczkowski, *Naziology* (Hebrew) (Jerusalem: HaSifriyah HaZionit HaKtana, 1944). Buczkowski believes that nationalism is a consequence of external

social and cultural pressures. In his opinion, the Great Wall of China and the isolation of many regions of Asia deterred the crystalization of nationalism.

See also: Shabbtai Rosenne, "Nationality Law and the Law of Return," *Journal de Droit Internationale*, 1954. Rosenne analyzes the Law of Return prior to the amendment of 1970 and raises several alternatives for the definition of "who is a Jew" for the purpose of the law. Among these is a proposal to adopt the idea of the country that casts out the Jew. This person would be considered a Jew for the purpose of leaving the country but would not be considered a Jew in the country receiving him (Israel).

18. High Court of Justice (Supreme Court's Division) File 58/68, Benjamin Shalit v. Minister of the Interior, *ILR*, vol. 23 (2), p. 608ff.

19. High Court of Justice (Supreme Court's Division) File 563/77, Eileen Dorflinger v. Minister of the Interior, *ILR*, vol. 33 (2) p. 97.

20. Law of Return (Amendment no. 1) 5730–1970, *ILB*, 886, p. 34.

21. *Ha'Aretz* of 6 February 1970.

22. Quotation from halacha regarding the conditions for conversion. Moshe HaLevi Steinberg, *Hukat HaGer/The Law of the Convert* (Jerusalem: R. Moss Publications, 5739–1971). *ET, s.v.* "Ger" (convert), vol. 6, pp. 253–89.

The stipulations for a person undergoing conversion proceedings according to religious law are as follows: (a) taking upon oneself the yoke of Torah and Commandments and the desire to partake of the collective responsibility for the Jewish people; (b) circumcision; (c) ritual bath purifying the person from his Gentile status and the pronouncing of a prayer.

23. High Court of Justice (Supreme Court's Division), File 230/86, Shoshana (Susan) Miller v. the Minister of the Interior and others, decision: 2 December 1986 (not yet published).

24. High Court of Justice (Supreme Court's Decision) File 113/84, Haggit Bankovsky v. Haifa District Rabbinic Tribunal, *ILR*, vol. 39 (3), p. 365. In this case a woman was converted in Israel following a strict Orthodox ritual. Her conversion was terminated after the woman confessed to having driven a car on the Sabbath and to not obeying ritual dietary laws. As a result, her marriage to her Jewish husband was declared as void "ab initio."

25. *Ha'Aretz* of 28 January 1970 and 2 February 1970 concerning "the mobile Rabbinical Court of Conversion" established by the Chief Orthodox Rabbinate in Israel.

26. Moshe HaLevi Steinberg, *Hukat HaGer/The Law of the Convert*, pp. 247–48. Michael Corinaldi, "The Personal Status of the Karaites" (Jerusalem: R. Mass Publications, 6744–1984).

27. *Ha'Aretz* of 28 January 1970.

28. American Jewish (non-Orthodox) leadership showed a great lack of understanding when referring to the Shoshana Miller precedent as "a victory for pluralism." Rabbi Charles Kroloff, president of the Association of Reform

Zionists, called the ruling "a giant step forward for religious pluralism in Israel" (*Stark Jewish News*, Canton, Ohio, January 1987).

In practical as well as constitutional terms, nothing changed. Being accepted as a Jew, as far as the repatriation is concerned, does not mean being Jewish enough to marry a Jew in Israel, or to be buried in a Jewish cemetery, or even to deliver testimony in a family court. If the Orthodox establishment were certain that the existing law forbids Miller and others like her from enjoying the benefit of automatic Israeli citizenship, they would not have launched a campaign to adjust the law to their need years before the Miller affair occurred (by demanding a change in the Law of Return to sanction the Orthodox conversion as the only conversion valid for obtaining Israeli citizenship for converts).

29. Yitzhak Artzi, "Secular Jewish Nationality—A Body without a Soul," *Temuroth* (monthly), March 1970, p. 19.

30. *Ha'Aretz* of 28 January 1970.

31. The new trend of accepting Orthodoxy as a common national denominator contradicts the basic understanding of the secular founders of political Zionism.

Arthur Ruppin, *Milchemet HaYehudim L'kiyum/The Jews Fight for Their Survival* (Tel Aviv: Bialik Institute, 1940) states: "A man belongs to the same nation, i.e., the same national group, to which he feels most connected by history, culture and common customs."

Eliezer Ben Yehudah, the genius who renewed the Hebrew language, expressed his view on a nation (*oomah* in Hebrew): "A community of joint origin, of common mother tongue, of common history and to some extent, gathered in one territory" (as quoted by Justice Berenson in the Ruffeisen case, p. 2452).

Justice Haim Herman Cohen expressed his opinion by stating: "Hitler denied the right of Jewish identity as part of our personal choice. It is our duty to restore this human right" (*Ma'ariv* of 6 September 1964).

David Ben-Gurion, Israel's first prime minister, was the first to understand the real meaning of the amendment to the Law of Return, stating that "this action . . . will cause a rift within the Jewish people" (*LaMerchav* of 13 February 1970).

Jacob L. Talmon, in his dissertation on "who is a Jew," takes another stand. He defends the majority vote in the Ruffeisen case by stating that "till the spread of Nazi racism adoption of a non-Jewish religion had been an act of abjuring the common [Jewish] state. Hitler is thus, indirectly, the author of that intractable religious-national situation, which may become quite impossible if, as is so ardently desired by Zionists, Soviet Russia lifts the ban on emigration of her Jews to Israel. The Jewish State would then be flooded by tens of thousands of Jews whose marriages and births have no legitimacy in the eyes of Rabbinic law." Boas Evron, *A National Reckoning* (Tel Aviv: Dvir Publishing House,

1988). Jacob Neusner, *Judaism in the Secular Age—Essays on Fellowship, Community and Freedom* (New York: Utav Publishing House, 1970).

32. Benjamin Akzin, *The Declaration of Independence of the State of Israel,* the Jubilee Book in honor of Pinhas Rosen, ed. Haim Cohen (Jerusalem: Mifal Shikhpul, 1962), p. 52.

33. The Nuremberg Racial Laws were enacted by the Reichstag (the German Parliament), in 1935 following Adolf Hitler's speech in the Reichstag. For the text of these laws see: *HaShoah B'Teud/ The Holocaust Documented* (Jerusalem: Yad VaShem, 5736).

34. Jean Paul Sartre, *Anti-Semite and Jew* (New York: Grove Press Inc., 1962).

35. Bills presented by Rabbi Meir Kahane to the Eleventh Knesset:

(1). Bill against Insult to Judaism, the Jewish People, Injury to the Land of Israel and the State of Israel and against Racism 5745–1984 (no. 123/331), in which racism is defined as follows: "Any claim of national, religious, or racial superiority, and the inability of a person who, meanwhile, is not part of the same nation, religion, or race to join them, yet claims of division, separation, or difference among nations will not be considered as racism." (Brought before the Knesset on 22 October 1984.)

(2). Bill for the Release of Jews Guilty of Nationalistic Actions Defined as Crimes, Offenses, or Sins 5745–1985 (no. 123/352). (Brought before the Knesset on 18 February 1985.)

(3). Bill against the Defamation of Judaism 5745–1985 (no. 123/525). (Brought before the Knesset on 22 July 1985.)

(4). Bill regarding Temple Mount 5745–1985 (no. 123/617), which deals with Jewish rule on Temple Mount by means of the Chief Rabbinate. (Brought before the Knesset on 17 February 1986.)

(5). Bill for Memorial Day for Spiritual Holocaust 5746–1986 (no. 123/642), which deals with the spiritual holocaust—cultural religious persecution—that occurred in the State of Israel, as believed by the bill's author. This Memorial Day for Spiritual Holocaust would serve as a date for memorializing the destruction of religious Judaism in Israel. (Brought before the Knesset on 7 April 1986.)

(6). Bill to Halt the Construction of the Mormon Missionary Center 5746–1985 (no. 123/577). (Brought before the Knesset on 23 December 1985.)

(7). Two bills presented by Rabbi Kahane in November 1985 to the Knesset (as a matter of coincidence, exactly fifty years after the Third Reich enacted racist regulations concerning Jews in Germany). One of the draft bills was labeled, "The Law of Authority in Israel," following almost exactly Maimonides' Laws of Kings 1:4, which states that "a king shall not be appointed in Israel unless his mother is Jewish . . . and not only as King, but in any position of authority in Israel. . . . All appointments shall be from among your brethren." Speaker of the Parliament invalidated these drafts as racist and Rabbi Kahane condemned the Knesset of actions against Judaism.

The official organ of the Lubavitcher Rabbi in Israel (Kfar Habbad) expressed its support for Kahane's efforts as far as they follow the Torah rulings (*Kol Ha'Ir* of 22 November 1985).

In an unprecedented action, 47 members of the prestigious Yad VaShem Institute (a research institute and archive on the Holocaust located in Jerusalem) sent the following letter to the Press:

> We, members of the staff of Yad VaShem . . . hereby express our shock and abhorrence at the racial incitement being expounded upon by Rabbi Meir Kahane M.K. His venom recently found expression in two draft bills. . . . These bills resemble, both in content and in formulation, the infamous Nuremberg Laws adopted by Nazis. . . . Instead of the terms used in the Nazi Laws, Kahane uses terminology which comes from supposedly religious sources. But the result is the same: denial of a citizen's civil rights, his honor, and even existence because of his racial origins and/or his religious affiliation. (The *Jerusalem Post* of 18 November 1985)

36. Civil File 194–197/82 "John Doe" v. "Joan Doe" in the Jerusalem District Court (unpublished).

37. Justice Haim Cohen, *Ma'ariv*, 6 September 1964. Arthur Ruppin, *The Jews Fight For Their Survival* (Tel Aviv: Bialik Institute, 1940) (Hebrew).

38. Amendment to the Law of Return, 5730–1970, *ILB*, p. 43.

39. Memorandum—Bill regarding the jurisdiction of Rabbinic Courts 5744–1983. This is a memorandum presented by the Ministry of Religious Affairs to fundamentally alter the existing legal situation, which was regulated in the Law of Jurisdiction of Rabbinic Courts (Marriage and Divorce) 5714–1953. The existing law was also deemed insignificant by those who hold with rule of law (versus religious rule). Criticism of the existing rule focused on several levels.

First, obligatory law necessitates rabbinic courts and religious law within the borders of the State of Israel and abroad, when both marriage partners are Jews and citizens or residents of Israel.

Second, rabbinic courts, established in accordance with the law, do not recognize religious Jewish law not of the Orthodox trend, thus causing discrimination towards non-Orthodox trends of Judaism and to isolated Orthodox groups such as the Karaites.

Third, although established under state rule, the rabbinic courts recognize international judicial incidence only as long as the parties do not need the rabbinic courts (i.e., claims for alimony and child maintenance under defined conditions). They are granted judicial recognition according to the obligatory general "civil" law of the State.

Fourth, religious courts adopted ritual prohibitions for themselves that were annulled by the Supreme Court of the State as opposing the principles of "freedom of conscience," which includes "freedom of action" (Supreme Court Case 80/ 63, *ILR*, vol. 16, p. 2408). In actuality, the former do not recognize the marriage of a Cohen (one of the priestly tribe) with a divorcee; they are adamant regarding the observance of *chalitza* (the act of removing the sandal of a brother-in-law, in the law of levirate); and obviously they do not recognize civil marriages, or religious marriages performed by Reform rabbis, nor do they recognize divorces performed by Conservative rabbis.

Finally, there exists in the rabbinic courts the openly declared inequality between the sexes. Women are unacceptable as witnesses (an indirect way has been found to bring their statements before the rabbinic court), and of course women are not permitted to serve as rabbinic judges.

The new bill thrusts halacha deeper into the field of justice, breaking down the remnants of the rule of law with regard to personal status and other areas. For example:

(1). One who is not a Jew, but who is married to a Jew, would be subservient to the rabbinic court. The jurisdiction of the religious courts would injure non-Jewish parties, forcing upon them the right of the Gentile spouse to a fair trial before a judicial instance that is meaningless to the religious courts due to the court's non-Jewish religious origin.

(2). It is enough for one of the spouses in Israel to be accidentally discovered in order to bestow jurisdiction on the rabbinic court, even when neither of the litigants has any real connection with Israel.

(3). The Judaism of a spouse for the jurisdictional need is according to halacha and not according to the Law of Return; thus a "Jew in doubt" (including an apostate Jew, who does not even have a spark of Judaism in him) who for reasons of comfort or desirability or to irritate one's spouse, who would present a claim in Israel, would be granted a hearing.

(4). Contrary to the existing situation, couples married in civil ceremonies performed abroad, whether as civilians of Israel or prior to their immigration to Israel would lose their legitimacy unless approved by the religious courts, as the sole authority. This system is greatly doubted in light of the fact that it would harm international judicial principles, which until now Israel has taken pains to maintain, and it would also injure the couple's vested rights.

(5). In fact, all matters of alimony and child maintenance would be given over to religious authority.

(6). Of course the issue of "who is a Jew" would be solved, without having to amend the Law of Return. Conversion would not be valid in Israel for any matter unless it were recognized by the Orthodox rabbinic court. See also: Moshe Ben-Ze'ev, "Central Notice of Those Unfit for Marriage," *HaPraklit*, Issue C, vol. 30, p. 249.

40. Documents regarding the Ethiopians—PM Shimon Peres, Ministry of Absorption, and the Chief Rabbis.

Nadav Shraga, "One God in the Heavens and on Earth," *Ha'Aretz* of 24 September 1985. Gideon Samet, "Strange Sights across from the Dati-can," *Ha'Aretz* of 20 September 1985. Israel Eldard, "The Ethiopian Immigrants, Ritually Bathed in Blood," *Yedioth Aharonoth* of 19 July 1985.

Ephraim Isaac, himself an Ethiopian Jew residing permanently in the United States, furnished the Israeli government with a report in which he stated:

> It may appear ironic to those who do not know the cult of Ethiopian Jews that the required "immersion" is seen by them as a Christian ritual, hence the vehement objection to it. Interestingly and not inaccurately, the word used to translate the Hebrew *tebila* by most Ethiopian Jews in Israel now is not the Ethiopian *tabel*, religious-medicinal water (frequent purification), but *temqat*, a normally one-time sacramental baptism practiced by Christians. Historically Ethiopian Jews have known involuntary *temquat*, hence . . . in Israel shy away from even swimming in public fearing that under the present conditions it may amount to involuntary Christianization. ("The Absorption of Ethiopian Jews in Israel—A JDC Consultation Report," June 2–30, 1985, Princeton, New Jersey.)

41. Law of Child Adoption, 5741–1971, *ILB*, 1028 of 28 May 1981.

42. Law of Religious Jewish Services 5731–1971, *ILB*, p. 130. Criminal Appeal case 427/64, Ya'ir v. Minister of Religion, ILR, 19 (3), p. 403. "Details on the Burial of Israeli Spy, Wolfgang Lutz's Wife," *Ma'ariv* of 26 June 1973.

For a general view of burial limitations in Israel see: Shmuel Gilboa, "Dying Free in Our Land," *Yedioth Aharonoth* of 1 January 1986.

Chapter Five: Back to the Ghetto

1. Akiva Ernst Simon, "Totalitarianism and Anti-Totalitarianism" in *HaZ'chut Lichanech, Chovah Lichanech/The Right to Educate, The Obligation to Educate* (Tel Aviv: Sifriyat HaPoalim, 5743), pp. 113–44, especially 128–29 on duplicty in the Jewish world. Irving Howe, ed., *Revisited—Totalitarianism in Our Century* (Tel Aviv: Sifriyat HaPoalim, 1984).

2. George Orwell, *1984* (New York: Signet, 1982).

3. Milovan Djilas, *The New Class—A Study of Contemporary Communism* (Tel Aviv: Am-Oved Publishing House, 5718–1958) (Hebrew translation).

4. Jacob L. Talmon, *The Origins of Totalitarian Democracy* (London:

Secker and Warburg, 1952). (Hebrew translation, Dvir: Zmora Bitan Publishers, 1987).

5. Joseph Shamir, "The Curse of the Twentieth Century," in *1984—Mabat Sheyni—Totalitariut BaMe'ah Ha-20/1984—A Second Look—Totalitarianism in the Twentieth Century*, ed. Irving Howe (Tel Aviv: Sifriyat HaPoalim, 5743–1984).

6. As quoted by Amnon Rubinstein in *The Zionist Dream Revisited* (New York: Shocken Books, 1984), p. 160.

7. Yehoshafat Harkabi, *The Bar-Kokhba Syndrome, Risk and Realism in International Politics* (Chappaque, New York: Rossel Books, 1983).

8. Rubinstein, *The Zionist Dream Revisited*, p. 84.

Epilogue

1. The *Jerusalem Post* of 26 January 1986.

Bibliography

General

Djilas, Milovan. *The New Class: A Study of Contemporary Communism.* Tel Aviv: Am-Oved Publishing House, 1958. Hebrew version. London: Thames & Hudson, 1958. English edition.

Milosz, Czeslaw. *Zniewolony Umysl (The Captive Mind).* Paris: Institut Literacki Kultura, 1953. In Polish. New York: Vintage Books, 1966. English edition.

Orwell, George (Eric Blair). *1984.* New York: New American Library, 1962.

Talmon, Jacob L. *The Origins of Totalitarian Democracy.* Tel Aviv: Zmora-Bitan Publishers, 1987. Hebrew version. London: Secker and Vanburg, 1952. English edition.

Toynbee, Arnold. *The World and the West.* New York and London: Oxford University Press, 1953.

Judaism

Dimont, Max I. *Jews, God and History.* New York: New American Library, 1964.

Hirschberg, Harris H. *Hebrew Humanism.* Los Angeles: California Writers, 1964.

Leibovitz, Jehoshua. *On Belief, History and Values.* Jerusalem: Akademon 5752. In Hebrew.

Neusner, Jacob. *Judaism in the Secular Age, Essays on Fellowship, Community and Freedom.* Hoboken, N.J.: Ktav Publishing House, Inc.

Runes, Dagobert D. *Dictionary of Judaism*. New York: Citadel, 1959.

Strack, Herman L. *Introduction to the Talmud and Midrash*. New York: Atheneum, 1978.

State and Religion

Abramov, Zalman S. *Perpetual Dilemma: Jewish Religion in the Jewish State*. Cranbury, N.J.: University Press, 1976.

Aloni, Shulamit. *The Arrangement: From Rule of Law to Halachic Rule*. Tel Aviv: Othpaz, 1970. In Hebrew.

Englard, Yitzhak. *Incorporation of the Jewish Law in the Israeli Judicial System*. In *B'Haguth U'VHalacha (In Thought and in Halacha)*. Jerusalem: Dept. of Toraic Culture, Jewish Agency, Ministry of Education, 5728. In Hebrew.

Falk, Zeev W. *Law and Religion: The Jewish Experience*. Jerusalem: Mesharim Publishers, 1981.

Gottschalk, Alfred. *A Strategy for Non-Orthodox Judaism in Israel. Judaism* (Fall, 1962), p. 421.

Hareven, Alouph. *On the Difficulty of Being an Israeli*. Jerusalem: The Van Leer Jerusalem Foundation, 1983. In Hebrew.

Katz, Jacob. *Between Jews and Gentiles*. Jerusalem: Bialik Institute, 5721. In Hebrew.

Leslie, Clement S. *The Rift in Israel: Religious Authority and Secular Democracy*. London: Routledge & Kegan Paul, 1971.

Liebman, Charles S., and Eliezer Don Yehiya. *Civil Religion in Israel: Traditional Judaism and Political Culture in the Jewish State*. Berkeley: University of California Press, 1983.

Polish, David. *Renew Our Days: The Zionist Issue in Reform Judaism*. Jerusalem: World Zionist Organization and World Union for Progressive Judaism, 1976.

Reines, Alvin J. *Questions and Answers on Polydoxy*. St. Louis: Institute of Creative Judaism, n.d. Pamphlet.

Rubinstein, Ammon. *The Zionist Dream Revisited*. New York: Shocken Books, 1984.

Schiff, Gary S. *Tradition and Politics: The Religious Parties in Israel*. Detroit: Wayne State University Press, 1977.

Schweid, Eliezer. *Judaism and Secular Culture*. Tel Aviv: HaKibutz Ha'Meuchad, 1981. In Hebrew.

Shiloh, Samuel. *The Ruler's Law Is Binding (Dina d'Malkhuta dina)*. Jerusalem: Academy of Science, 5735. In Hebrew.

Who Is a Jew?

Agassi, Joseph. *Religion and Nationality: Towards an Israel National Identity.* Tel Aviv: Papyrus Publishing House, 1984. In Hebrew.

Ruppin, Arthur. *The Jews Fight for Their Survival.* Tel Aviv: Bialik Institute, 1960. In Hebrew.

Sartre, Jean-Paul. *Anti-Semite and Jew.* New York: Grove Press, 1962.

Shaky, Avner H. *Who Is a Jew in the Israeli Law.* 2 vols. Jerusalem: Institute for Family Law Research and the Rabbi Kook Institute, 1976. In Hebrew.

Shavit, Jacob. *From Hebrew to Canaanite: Aspects of the Hebrew Renaissance; from Radical Zionism to anti-Zionism.* Jerusalem: The Domino Press, 1984. In Hebrew.

Jewish Fundamentalism

Harkabi, Jehoshafat. *The Bar Kokhba Syndrome: Risk and Realism in International Politics.* Chappaqua, N.Y.: Rossel Books, 1983.

Rubinstein, Danny. *On the Lord's Side: Gush Emunim.* Tel Aviv: HaKibutz Ha'Meuchad Publishing House, 1982. In Hebrew.

Segal, Haggai. *Dear Brothers: The "Jewish Underground" Story.* Jerusalem: Keter Publishing House, 1987. In Hebrew.

Sprinzak, Ehud. *Gush Emunim: The Politics of Zionist Fundamentalism in Israel.* New York: American Jewish Committee, 1986.

Weiler, Gershon. *Jewish Theocracy.* Tel Aviv: Am-Oved Publishers, 1976. In Hebrew.